FIELDCRAFT, SNIPING
AND INTELLIGENCE

FIELDCRAFT, SNIPING
and INTELLIGENCE

By

MAJOR NEVILL A. D. ARMSTRONG
O.B.E., F.R.G.S.

Late Chief Reconnaissance Officer
Canadian Army

The Naval & Military Press Ltd

Published by

The Naval & Military Press Ltd

Unit 5 Riverside, Brambleside
Bellbrook Industrial Estate
Uckfield, East Sussex
TN22 1QQ England

Tel: +44 (0)1825 749494

www.naval-military-press.com
www.nmarchive.com

PREFACE

The author hopes this book may be of some value to Battalion Intelligence Officers and others who are primarily responsible for the training of Scouts, Observers and Snipers.

It was proved beyond question that the services rendered by the Battalion Intelligence Sections as established in the Great War of 1914-18 were of incalculable value.

This fact formed the basis of a series of reports written by well-known divisional fighting generals and issued immediately after the Armistice—such references as " Eyes and ears of the Army " were used.

A fond hope was also cherished by those whose untiring efforts in the early days of the Great War helped to bring into being the establishment later known as the Battalion Intelligence Section, that post-war training of snipers, scouts and observers would not be forgotten : for there appeared to be a tendency among Army musketry men to scorn the sniper—they held that sniping was only a " phenomenon " of trench warfare and would not be likely to occur again.

Sniping *was* forgotten—as the years passed by telescopic sights disappeared from the Army and the Battalion Intelligence Section (1914-18) ceased to exist.

The few experts whose services were obtained to train young soldiers in the art of fieldcraft and sniping returned to the outposts of Empire whence they had come and were heard of no more.

Twenty-two years passed by and once again " In Flanders Fields " we fought the same foe—this time the sons of the veterans of 1914-18 trod in their fathers' footsteps.

Once again lives were sacrificed on the altar of the expert Hun sniper ; we were not ready—we had forgotten our lesson.

The author dedicates this book to the memory of that intrepid band of hunters, scouts and snipers who were members of the Battalion Intelligence Sections of the British Expeditionary Force in 1914-18.

FOREWORD

BY

COLONEL LORD COTTESLOE, C.B., V.D., T.D.

The hunter of big game at home or abroad has learnt by experience not only to make certain of the shot he fires, but to approach his objective unseen, to observe tracks and signs and all else within his ken, and to tackle unforeseen emergencies. Such a man has acquired in a high degree the qualifications of a very efficient individual soldier. What indeed is the human animal in war but a special variety of soft-skinned dangerous game ?

The number of skilled hunters in any country mainly depends on the extent of its woods and mountains. Thus, Scotland furnished its invaluable unit of Lovat's Scouts during the last war ; Central Europe trains a great quantity of experienced hunters ; Africa and the New World much larger numbers. Major Armstrong writes with a full experience of Canada in peace and of Flanders in war.

The static form of sniping, which chiefly prevailed in the last war, is likely to be exceptional in future ; the sniper needs to learn all the arts of concealed approach which the hunter and the scout practise. Much of these can be acquired by diligent training, though it takes a lifetime to make a Baden Powell or a Burnham. The scout-sniper is fighting a battle of wits with the enemy ; he must also be able to observe and to make a clear report of what he has seen, and must be a master in using his rifle with its telescope sight.

It is not generally known in this country how very widely the telescope sight is now in use by hunters in all parts of the world ; this is in fact a corollary of the very great accuracy which has been developed in modern rifles. Its sphere in war has been correspondingly enlarged.

Major Armstrong is a most experienced guide, whose practical advice will be of value to many. I wish all success to his book.

Cottesloe

SWANBOURNE.
November, 1940.

CONTENTS

LIST OF PLATES

xi

INTRODUCTION

THE BATTALION INTELLIGENCE SECTION, 1914-18

INTERNAL ECONOMY—TRAINING—ORGANIZATION

It is difficult to avoid repetition in a handbook of this nature, particularly when discussing Training and Organization, but it is thought that a few general remarks on the subjects above, even if slight repetition creeps in, will be helpful to the student.

Training.

In Brigade and Divisional Reserve the Battalion Intelligence and Scout Officers should carry on a system of training. No battalion work should interfere with these arrangements, as the time allotted for the training of the section during active service is very limited.

On account of the limited time, it was always suggested that, whenever possible, the Intelligence Section should be excused battalion duties such as guards and fatigues, and that every opportunity should be given to the scouts and snipers to meet and train together, to get to know each other well, particularly the scouts, and to more or less train each other and discuss their work and formulate plans for harassing the enemy, such as stealth raids, capturing posts, cutting wire, patrol formations and so on. For this reason the section should be billeted together and, if possible, live in dugouts by themselves, it being inadvisable to discuss projected stealth raids or any other important scout work with anyone outside the section.

Reports.

The observers and scouts should report everything they see and must be particularly well trained in this most important duty. The Intelligence Officer should go carefully over all the reports and pick out the useful from the useless information, separating such information as definite or indefinite.

Organization.

Battalions are responsible for collecting information about the ground between their positions and the enemy's positions and any obstacles in that area, for locating the position of the enemy's front line, and for information about that line.

Brigades should be responsible for locating the enemy's approaches, supports and secondary lines, and for all information pertaining to those lines ; also for the direction from which the enemy's batteries are firing, the position of any forward batteries, and for information concerning movements in rear of the enemy's lines.

Forwarding Information.

All ranks must be impressed with the necessity of forwarding information regarding the enemy's movements or special activity, or any definite identification, to the formation whom it concerns at the earliest possible moment, in addition to including the information in their daily report. When any operations take place which lead to the capture of prisoners or equipment, the identification, when possible, will be immediately forwarded by wire.

Records.

Brigade and Battalion Intelligence Officers should keep full records of all information regarding their frontage in the log books provided for that purpose.

Books for the use of observation posts should be marked with the name and number of the post, and log book or patrol books will be marked with the sector they cover.

All these books will be handed over on relief.

The Intelligence Section.

This section should be thoroughly acquainted with our own defences and organization, such as trench mortars, machine guns, sniping posts, observation posts, Battalion H.Q., Company H.Q., etc.

Lists of these locations must not be carried by observers or others in the front line or placed in posts or dugouts.

Special Intelligence.

When any unusual activity or any suitable target is observed in the enemy lines, the post making the observation will report immediately to the nearest unit which can make use of the information.

The distribution of and method of employing the Intelligence Section is discussed at some length in this handbook, but, generally speaking, the distribution depends much on local conditions and the general situation, whether it is trench or open warfare, the nature of the operation contemplated—defensive, offensive or stationary—the nature of the front, and so on.

In some instances more observers would be required, in others more scouts and fewer observers, in others a few snipers, etc. It depends on the general situation and local conditions, and the best distribution must be left to the discretion of the Battalion Intelligence Officer and Scout Officer.

Sniping Posts and Observation Posts.

Selected battalion snipers and special observers or spotters will occupy sniping and observation posts behind the lines.

Posts should be built by the snipers and observers who are to occupy them. These posts should be well concealed.

The map location of observation posts must be sent to Brigade H.Q.

Internal Economy.

The section should have good billets and live together and endeavour to promote a high state of *esprit de corps*.

They should be rationed from H.Q.

N.C.Os'. Special Duties.

1. To generally assist Intelligence Officer and act as quartermaster.
2. To make regular rounds of observation posts and sniping posts.
3. Routine.
4. Making out daily rosters.
5. Cleanliness of men, arms and equipment.
6. Distribution of rations.
7. Supervision of sniping and observation.
8. Collecting reports.
9. Overseeing construction of loopholes, hides and observation posts.
10. Taking out patrols.
11. Care of rifles and sights.
12. Concealment.
13. Reconnaissance and observation.

Equipment for Section.

1. Telescopic sights.
2. Telescopes and field-glasses.
3. Veils.
4. Snipers' suits.
5. Revolvers for scouts.
6. Watches.
7. Bicycles.
8. Gas helmets.
9. Notebook, pencil and rubber.
10. Map of enemy's front.

OBSERVATION

Intelligent and accurate observation is of immense value. Inaccurate observation and incorrect statements are of much danger.

Scouts require much training in observation and frequently act as observers.

Observers need not necessarily be scouts, but both require very similar training, particularly in map reading.

Snipers require to have keen observation and knowledge of scouting, but it is not important for them to be highly trained in other subjects.

It may so happen that a man who has proved himself to be an expert sniper can neither read nor write ; this may not be of much consequence in a sniper, but it is essential for a scout or observer to be well educated.

Training.

It has been suggested in some quarters that specialist training, so far as it pertains to scouts, observers and snipers, should be given separately. That is to say, special courses should be arranged for scouts, observers and snipers, and they should be trained separately.

Observers and Scouts.

It is difficult to draw any clearly defined line between observers and scouts concerning their training ; their qualifications are very similar and they should be trained together.

Snipers.

It is admissible that it might be better to train snipers specially ; although good shooting is necessary, it is by no means the only qualification. Special courses of short duration could be arranged, etc. In any event, observation, scouting and sniping are closely allied and difficult to separate one from the other for training purposes.

Observation and the ability to describe what he has seen are most important qualifications in an observer or scout.

Observers.

Must be trained in the following subjects :—
> Use of telescope and field-glasses.
> What to look for, etc., and how to look for it.
> Construction of observation posts.
> Landscape sketching.
> Map reading and mapping.
> Knowledge of aeroplane photographs.
> Use of compass.
> Protective colour.
> Front-line Intelligence system, and log maps.
> Judging distance.

Aids.

There are certain aids to observation—

> Telescope ;
> Field-glasses ;
> Periscopes ;
> Your own eyes.

If given the choice, select a telescope. For concentrated detail it is unequalled, and it is far easier to conceal. Field-glasses are very good, but for concentration they are greatly excelled by a good telescope.

Selection of Men.

In order to be of any benefit to a battalion and to warrant the special and careful training given to them, men to act as specialists should be carefully selected by their officers or N.C.Os., and in no case should they be detailed (by numbers, so to speak) to attend a specialist course, or any other course for that matter.

Men must be highly trained to become expert observers, and no time should be wasted in an effort to train illiterate or unsuitable men.

The Adjutant of every battalion should apply for a syllabus of the training carried on at all important schools where men of his battalion may be sent. This applies in a marked degree to specialist schools.

Company Commanders dislike parting with really good and efficient men even temporarily, and in the past have detailed men to attend schools because they may be undisciplined and a general nuisance to the company, have bad eyesight, be deaf or lazy, and for many other causes. This practice is unfair to the men and to those detailed to train them, and the battalion which repeatedly sends a poor type of man to important schools very quickly earns a bad name for itself, as men of other units are apt to judge the discipline and smartness of the whole battalion from the character of the man it sends to schools. And the judgment has generally proved to be correct.

Important Qualifications.

1. Good eyesight—if possible, quick sight ; some men are born with this, others acquire it. In any event, observers, scouts and snipers must try to develop this quality. The eyes should always be restless when in the field. Try to develop animal sight, or from flank to flank.

2. Should not be colour blind or deaf.

3. Should be keen and intelligent.

4. Persistent, patient and plucky.

5. It is doubtful if men of an excitable nature will make good observers ; probably give their position away very soon.

6. Must be truthful.

Testing for Sight.—Before taking an observer into the Intelligence Section, his sight should be tested both by **day** and **night.** Men who have excellent daylight sight may be blind by night. Night observation is important.

Men should not be detailed for important work without regard to their ability to carry out the work.

Generally, try to select men who have led an out-of-door life, preferably in the woods, such as—

> Game hunters,
> Trappers,
> Prospectors,
> Surveyors,
> Lumberjacks,
> Poachers, etc.

There are many reasons why this type of man should train very quickly as observer, scout, etc. The majority of them have a good deal of common sense and, of necessity, good practical knowledge and initiative, being trained to use their wits when in places sometimes remote from civilization. They move silently ; their food and living has frequently depended upon success with eyes, rod and rifle. It is therefore essential for them to be particularly observant, patient and persistent, and, by nature of their calling, they are usually brave men.

I have dwelt at considerable length on the question of the selection of men because the importance of it is so much misunderstood as a general rule even by officers employing specialists.

Position.

Observers must have a good eye for ground, and great care should be exercised in the selection of an observation post, particularly if it is a brigade or corps observation post and if it is known that this post will be occupied for some considerable period.

System.

A certain system should be adopted when scouting for an observation post. It is of very little use going off " into the blue," hoping a good one will fall out of the sky.

(a) Ascertain flanks of battalion or brigade frontage.

(b) Procure telescope.

(c) Observe carefully when coming under observation.

(d) Dawn is the best time, but be careful of rising sun if you face East.

(e) Reconnoitre entire frontage unless it is known that a certain portion is unsuitable.

(f) Examine enemy country carefully from each point, taking notes of best field of view.

(g) Look for concealment in preference to protection first of all, because good concealment is protection.

(h) Do not be in too great a hurry ; it is most important to locate good position and not always an easy matter.

Note.—During the period of open warfare in 1918 (the last ninety days) it was found particularly difficult to get men to locate really good positions. Sometimes it was impossible to obtain any view at all.

The rapidity of advance made intelligent observation difficult. When I say "intelligent observation," I mean that observation is of little value unless followed by quick action. Advantage must be taken of observation. In order to do this, it is imperative to have communication with the right people, and a system, particularly if artillery fire co-operation is called for ; and in the majority of cases in a rapid advance the observers report artillery targets.

Observers selected for an expected rapid advance must of all things be particularly expert in map reading and taking bearings with compass and protractor, and in writing reports legibly and accurately. This is by no means an easy matter.

Make it Comfortable.

All posts, particularly observation posts, should be made reasonably comfortable, particularly if they cannot be relieved at frequent intervals. It is impossible for men to carry on efficiently if they are suffering much bodily discomfort.

How to Look or Observe.

Practical experience and common sense will alone make a proficient observer. It is very difficult to discuss this subject adequately in a book—so much depends on practical experience and demonstration—but it might be well to take a few hints from methods employed by hunters of game who naturally, to be successful, must know many things and must be keenly observant. Therefore we will divide up a few remarks under the following heads :—

1. Habits.
2. Signs.
3. Movement.
4. Protective Colour.

1. Habits.—To be successful, a game hunter must always study the habits of his animals. If he does not he can never hunt successfully.

First of all he must pin them down ; that is to say, he must be sure there is game in the country. He must be sure that he does not waste too much time and energy in observing nothing, so to speak, or waiting for things which will never appear.

It is quite simple to successfully observe and procure game when once a hunter knows how to study habits.

Our young observer must therefore get some idea of his enemy's habits—

(a) What time he gets up in the morning.

(b) What time he may be seen moving about.

(c) If he moves about at dawn.

(d) Whether his working parties go out at daylight.

(e) Whether he, like animals, rests at midday.

(f) Best time to find him in the evening.

A good observer will guarantee to show anyone a Boche at some period of the day, and usually will specify the time of day ; this refers to trench warfare principally.

4

Having studied the habits of his game for some time, the hunter feels more satisfied ; he has more confidence in himself and his ability as an observer.

This kind of observation is most necessary when sniping.

2. Signs, Tracks and Trails.—Signs are most important for the sniping observer. Like animals, your game will have particular tracks or trails to or from his working places, the animal to or from his feeding ground, etc. Frequently these trails will take your game over exposed places where he may be wholly or partially visible, and the hunter will get in his shot if the observation has been good.

The hunter will observe various tracks and trails leading to a dead carcase, and therefore prepares traps to capture or kill the animals in the night. We do a very similar thing. From aeroplane photos we observe tracks and trails leading to and from ration dumps, R.E. dumps, dugouts, trenches, etc., and these places are harassed with fire during the night.

WATER HOLES.—Animals frequently visit the same pond or lake and follow certain tracks. Also game frequently crosses streams at the same place. We frequently get water out of the same shell hole, or cross streams on bridges or the same bridge. Your observer has spotted this and puts his sniper on the target, and the hunter in the same way knows where to go for his game.

The observation of these signs, tracks and trails is vitally important if one is to be an expert observer, and a study of aeroplane photos will quickly prove the importance of tracks and trails.

3. Movement.—Observers as well as scouts must understand the danger of movement in giving away the enemy's position as well as their own. Hundreds of good observation posts have been given away by careless movement or general carelessness, not only in going to and from observation posts, but while these places are in occupation.

4. Protective Colour.—The good observer, like the good scout or sniper, must be trained if possible in the intelligent use of camouflage in order that he may be able to detect it when used by the enemy.

In trench or stationary warfare the use of protective colour has been brought to a very high state of perfection, and unless a man is particularly observant and knows what to look for he will never be able to spot important camouflage.

No amount of lecturing is of much avail when dealing with this subject ; it must be demonstrated practically.

LIGHT AND SHADOW.—The study of light and shadow is of great importance to the accomplished observer. Shadow will distort an object to the weirdest shapes and appearance, likewise light at certain angles. If the observer is not perfectly certain as to the nature of certain objects, it is well to examine them both in the morning and evening light.

What to Look For.

The remarks up to the present have dealt with *how* to look. Now it is necessary to give the observer some idea as to what to look for.

In trench warfare, if the observer is new at the game, it is advisable for him to make a note in his book of a few important things he must be on the look out for. It has been my experience that a great number of observers have very good sight, but do not know how to make use of it.

It is not always the obvious target that is important ; it is work which is being done, or positions, or movement which the enemy tries to conceal.

Important Information (Trench Warfare).

1. Observation posts, snipers' posts, loopholes of any kind.

2. Machine-gun emplacements.

3. Trench mortars (locate from flash and photos).

4. Smoke betraying dugouts.   Important H.Q. buildings, etc.

5. Working parties ; strength, time and place.

6. Trenches, position of new ones. Those being repaired or strengthened. Whether communicating trenches are organized for defence. Photos help.

7. **Wire.**—Where it has been made particularly strong or dug in, any gaps, the effect of our artillery fire on enemy's wire, also any wire behind front line, etc.

8. **Listening Posts.**—Scouts usually responsible for the location of these, but observers can keep their eyes open at **dawn** and **dusk.**

9. **Saps.**—Most important to keep careful watch on all new saps. Construction of these usually means attack.

10. **Mine.**—Unusual amount of soil spread out and probably camouflaged. Blue clay appearing in certain districts is almost a certain indication that excavation of some sort is proceeding.

Continuous pumping day and night.

Indication of steam or mist arising in the same place daily ; sound ranging.

11. **Trench Tramways.**—Usually rely on aero photos, but the observer should locate the actual position if possible by direct observation with the aid of the photo.

12. **Roads.**—Most important for observers to know the names of all important roads and their exact position on the map, particularly cross-roads, because in many cases pillboxes have been established at cross-roads. Movement seen on roads and nature of movement of immense importance. Also, besides roads, any lines of approach to the trenches, tracks used by reliefs, transport, etc.

13. **Aircraft.**—Generally whether they have been active and flying low and shooting up the trenches.

14. **Strong Points.**—Anything of suspicious nature resembling a strong point, redoubts, defended localities. Take bearings and compare with photo.

15. **Identification.**—Difficult to obtain ; identification of any unit by observation of cockades, bands, colour of uniform, etc., not reliable.

16. **Movement.**—Unusual movement in back areas by the enemy and movement of small parties of men in and around the trenches, if observed about dusk, will frequently foreshadow a relief. The observer should state if the men are carrying packs and rifles and the direction in which they are moving.

This information, together with that obtained from a prisoner taken about the same date, may be of much value.

17. **Dugouts.**—Watch carefully for any sign of dugouts given away carelessly by men or smoke and compare with photo of same locality.

18. **Artillery.**—Direction of fire, calibre of gun and extent of shelling. Our shells falling short, and enemy's falling short behind his own lines.

Artillery should be observed day and night. Observation of artillery fire is more usually observed and reported by battalion observers in support trenches and by brigade and corps observation posts.

Artillery liaison officers are informed of all enemy shelling and take action.

19. **Lights and Signals.**—Include flares sent up by the enemy and ourselves ; most important on certain occasions. Particularly S.O.S. signals.

> Searchlights ;
> Heliograph ;
> Visual, etc. ;
> Wireless installations ;
> Espionage.

20. **Dead Ground.**—Always report and watch approaches to any dead ground, particularly if this should be in No Man's Land or in immediate neighbourhood of enemy's front line.

21. Always report any information concerning the enemy, no matter how trivial it may seem to the observer.

22. **Dummy Trees.**—Were manufactured with very great success by special works R.Es. during trench warfare and were rarely spotted by the enemy.

23. **Dummy Men.**—It will require particularly proficient observation to spot the use of dummy men if these figures are carefully exposed. The Battalion observer is the man to depend upon for this, also the sniper in particular.

The enemy makes frequent use of dummy heads to draw fire, etc.

24. **Grass.**—Dummy grass of all shades can be so well manufactured to-day that it is difficult for the most expert observer either on the ground or in the air to locate it.

It is difficult for the expert in aeroplane photos to be certain either, if the grass has been carefully erected.

The observer is greatly helped by carelessness on the part of the enemy in detecting these things.

In Open Warfare : Attack.

In open warfare, when rapid advances are made in a few hours, it is difficult to control observation in battalions.

Every Man His Own Observer.—Every man in the front line during the advance practically becomes his own observer ; small units deal with the result of their own observation. Individual men have to deal with the result of their own information and observation. Here again is the necessity for observation and action.

Observation and Action.—In the attack, if a machine-gun nest is met with, observers or others cannot, as in trench warfare, report the location of this machine-gun post to H.Q. and wait for artillery or trench mortars to knock it out. On the contrary, they must use their own initiative and, with the aid of scouts and good observation, etc., the nest must be outflanked or rushed.

Communications.—Also during a rapid advance it has been impossible for front-line troops to make known the result of their observation in time for immediate action by other arms operating in their rear. They must depend upon whatever troops or tanks are operating in their immediate area.

Spotting Machine Guns.—Experienced battalion observers should be useful in the attack in quickly spotting the location of machine guns and pointing them out to snipers and others. Machine guns are the weapons to be most dreaded in open warfare, and unless the position is a particularly strong one these machine-gun nests must be dealt with by the infantry acting on their own initiative.

Observation of Enemy Snipers.—The enemy is nearly always active in sniping and causes numerous casualties. It should be the endeavour of our observers to try to locate these men or the direction of their fire and point out these targets to any soldier or sniper who may be close at hand, or the observer may be a good shot himself and deal with the result of his observation.

Likely Positions.—The observer in open warfare must have his wits about him as well as his eyes, and know where to look for the enemy. He must have a good eye for ground. Must not forget trees, buildings, church towers, commanding positions, flanking fire, windmills, sunken roads, roads generally, camouflage, pits dug in the open ground, farming implements scattered about, grain fields, long grass, fallen trees.

Own Initiative.—Observers during a rapid advance must be left largely to themselves to do the best they can ; they must report any information of importance at once to Battalion H.Q., and should keep careful watch for counter-attacks, or anything of an unusual or unexpected nature which may develop, particularly watching their flanks and reporting position, etc.

Brigade Observers.—The value of brigade observers in the attack depends to a large extent on the nature of the country over which troops are fighting and advancing. Command of view is essential, and in these days of rapid advances good observation posts have to be abandoned by the forward troops almost as soon as they are established.

During the Battle of Amiens brigade observation posts were established as soon as our attack slowed down when we reached trenches and wire. Many of these observation posts were established in trees, and in some cases our men reoccupied old Boche observation posts in trees, which is not always a wise proceeding.

During the Battle of Arras observation was good after Monchy le Preux had been taken.

Corps Observers.—Wherever possible Corps observers should establish three observation posts across the Corps frontage—one on the left, one in the centre, and one on the right. During the Battle of Amiens long-range observation was extremely difficult until the last phases of the fight, but at Arras observation was excellent and much important movement was observed.

Nature of Information.—Hostile artillery activity in the forward area, as well as in rear areas, and the nature of this activity. It is important to observe the nature of hostile artillery in the attack. It indicates several things—

Strength of his artillery.

Calibre of gun.

Whether he is withdrawing his long-range guns.

The depth of his long-range fire behind our front line and nature of projectile.

Nature of barrage, if any.

Whether the fire appears to be well controlled or erratic.

If he is using gas shells.

9

Night Bombing.—Position and extent of night bombing raids in the forward area.

Signals.—S.O.S. signals and lights of every description. During the attack, particularly in the early morning or at dusk, the most acute observation should be directed towards signals from our front-line troops.

Officers in the front line reported that on many occasions their signals were not observed or the artillery was slow in responding. This referred principally to the lengthening of our barrage when it was falling among our own troops.

Movement.—The Corps observation posts are able to report an immense amount of movement by road and railway behind the enemy's line : not only individual movement, but movement of large bodies of troops and guns and transport of every description.

Wireless.—These Corps observation posts being in communication by wireless with Corps heavy artillery, advantage was taken of all good targets reported.

Troops.—These observation posts were on many occasions able to report the various phases of an attack and extent of opposition.

NOTE.—The attack on Greenland Hill (during Battle of Arras) by the 51st Division was a wonderful sight and was watched by two of our Corps observation posts, as well as by all our troops who were attacking to the north of Monchy. A particularly heavy barrage was laid down by the enemy the moment the 51st reached the skyline or top of the hill.

Smoke.—Smoke denoting explosions or burning dumps and villages was continually reported.

Balloons.—Position and bearing of balloons.

Finally, men must be taught to observe **intensely,** particularly so in trench warfare.

They must be **systematic**—take small sections at a time.

They must not wander aimlessly about all over the country, which is a common fault.

Search their own wire, No Man's Land, and Boche wire.

Look with suspicion upon everything.

Keep enemy under constant observation.

Place themselves mentally in enemy's position.

Think what they would do under similar conditions.

Match cunning with cunning.

The importance of intelligent and accurate observation, coupled with quick action, cannot be too strongly impressed on all ranks, whether they be qualified observers or not.

Siting of Observation Posts.

The general proceeding to be employed when scouting for an observation post position has already been stated.

1. Do not establish an observation post in very close proximity to an occupied dugout. In one instance an observation post was built immediately over the entrance ; this is more than foolish and should never be allowed.

2. Sniping posts should not be established close to a battalion observation post.

3. Do not use new observation posts too soon after construction ; wait a couple of days and let them weather down.

4. Do not smoke or have fires in observation posts, or light candles ; use Tommy Cookers on the floor if necessary.

5. Do not forget to use gags and curtains in observation posts, and be careful to pull the curtain down behind you before pulling out gag. Sandbagging is bad to use as curtain ; the light shows through. A ground sheet is excellent.

6. Do not forget when facing the sun to be most careful about object glass flashing and giving position away.

Approach and Movement.

The greatest care should be exercised when entering or leaving an observation post. This precaution applies whether the observation post is under direct observation by the enemy from the ground or air.

It is waste of time to prepare and camouflage an observation post if the observers make a well-beaten track from their dugout to their observation post without any attempt at concealment from the air ; many an enemy observation post has been spotted by this means.

Exclusiveness.

This is most difficult to maintain, particularly when posts are either in or very close to the front line.

They are frequently betrayed through idle curiosity.

Post should be used exclusively by observers. This should be a Battalion Order, particularly as regards visitors in the line.

The greatest carelessness occurs sometimes when there is an artillery shoot on to knock out a trench-mortar position, etc. The liaison officer is allowed to select the best observation post for the job, and frequently invites officers from Brigade H.Q. or any other pals to come down and " see the fun."

What happens is this. The observation post is usually small, barely room for two men. There are three sightseers, not including artillery officer and observer on duty ; they all attempt to get inside, the curtain is pulled up and held by the officers who are partially inside and outside, cigarettes are being smoked, and the approach to observation post is under direct observation. Later, probably next day, the post is bombarded by " minnies " and two observers killed.

This is not an imaginary instance ; it actually occurred. Be particularly careful when snow is on the ground.

Diagram to explain the Organization and Method of employing the Corps Observers in Open Warfare.

As already stated, during the early phases of open warfare at Amiens distant observation was very difficult owing to the nature of the country, but at Arras and on to Mons observation was good.

Three observation posts were established across the Corps frontage as shown in the following diagram. Whenever possible each observation post was supplied with a German-speaking other rank in addition to its observers, to watch for and interrogate stray prisoners marching to the cages.

Communication between observation posts and H.Q. Corps Survey Section report centre was by wireless, ground wire, motor cycle, cycle or runner.

DIAGRAM ILLUSTRATING ARRANGEMENTS MADE DURING OPERATIONS FOR THE EMPLOYMENT OF CORPS SURVEY SECTION.

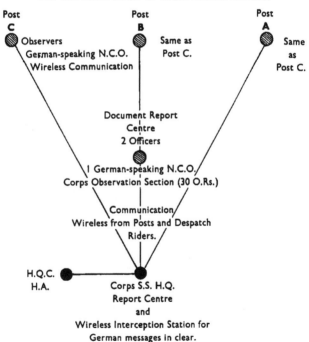

Post C — Observers, German-speaking N.C.O., Wireless Communication
Post B — Same as Post C.
Post A — Same as Post C.

Document Report Centre
2 Officers
1 German-speaking N.C.O.
Corps Observation Section (30 O.Rs.)
Communication
Wireless from Posts and Despatch Riders.

H.Q.C. H.A.
Corps S.S. H.Q. Report Centre
and
Wireless Interception Station for German messages in clear.

12

SCOUTING

Incidents in History.

It has been said, and correctly, that there is scarcely a battle in history which has not been lost or won in proportion to the value of the previous reconnaissance.

The great Duke of Marlborough was a good scout himself, and was so impressed with the value of skilful reconnaissance that even when he was a General commanding a large force he frequently went out on his own account as a scout to secretly reconnoitre the enemy's movements.

Cromwell, too, one of the greatest and most practical of all cavalry leaders, had officers styled " Scout Masters " whose business it was to collect all possible information regarding the enemy through scouts and spies. Much of his success in war was traceable to the previous knowledge of the enemy's moves thus gained.

Instances of important results from one scout's work are innumerable in history. Perhaps the most notable was the Battle of Sadorna, where a single scout of the German Army discovered the whole of the enemy's (Austrian) Army in a quite unexpected place. The German Army was turned that night into the new direction, and next day a battle was fought which decided the whole campaign.

Again, in the Franco-German War of 1870 another German scout discovered an Army Corps of the French in an unexpected place, unsupported by other troops. Acting on his information, the Germans were able to surround this force and destroy it.

In recent times, during the Battle of the Somme, when the Canadians were attacking Courcelette, two battalion scouts reported that the German trenches in front of the village were only being held by a few scattered sentries, whereas it was supposed to be held in force. Instead of waiting to advance until the next day, the infantry pushed ahead that night and captured Courcelette. This information doubtless saved hundreds of casualties.

Definition of a Scout.

A man trained to observe and procure information ; also highly trained in the use of ground. He must not use his weapon except in order to achieve his object.

Qualifications.

Scouts should not be too big or heavy. They should be quick and alert both in brain and movement.

Scouts require more specialized training than snipers in—

Map reading ;
Map making ;
Sketching ;
Reporting ;

particularly in memory sketching, which is most important.

It is not always possible for a scout to sit down and make a sketch on the spot ; he must sketch quickly or memorize.

Selection of Men.

Platoon and Company Commanders should be as careful as possible in their selection of men to act as scouts ; the safety of a whole brigade or division may sometimes depend on the information acquired by a single scout.

Men selected must be—

> Intelligent ;
> Tireless, courageous, cool, cautious ;
> Truthful ;
> Not colour-blind ;
> Have good eyesight ;
> Have acute hearing.

Not only should every scout have **pluck,** but this quality should be coupled with discretion and self-reliance.

It requires more pluck for a scout to go into danger alone than to " hop the bags " in company with all his pals ; he cannot very well turn back then.

A good scout knows the danger, knows he can turn back if he wants to and no one will be any wiser, but he does not do it as a rule.

Untrained Officers and Men.

If possible no officer or man should, except under exceptional circumstances, be permitted " to go over the parapet " for the purpose of carrying out reconnaissance work without previous training. When taking out new men for the first time while on active service, it is very inadvisable to rush them over in close proximity to the enemy's lines at once.

It is far better to take them out for the first night or two and keep them fairly close to their own trenches or positions ; allow them to get used to being out in No Man's Land in the dark.

If this is done, men gain confidence in themselves and will make good scouts. The Scout Officer or N.C.O. can keep careful observation of the behaviour of all new men while actually working in the danger zone, and will soon " spot " any man who obviously gets his " wind up " without any cause or who cannot see in the dark.

After the first night or two these new men can be worked over gradually towards the enemy lines.

During this time they must be keenly observant to locate their position and surroundings so that at any time they can reach their own lines in safety.

There are many authentic instances of officers and men walking directly into the German lines, having completely lost their bearings.

Scouting and **Observation** should go hand in hand together, because a good scout must be an expert in observation. But it does not necessarily follow that a good observer must be a good scout.

Scouting and Game Hunting.

Scouting in warfare is not at all unlike big game hunting, except that one is hunting the most formidable of all game, human beings. No matter how ferocious an animal may be, the hunter can usually afford to take chances by exposing himself or following up wounded game, etc.; but it is a different proposition when the hunter is confronted with a quarry who is armed with the most effective modern firearms and that deadly " thinking bullet."

Trench Warfare.

In trench warfare the habits of men very much resemble animals in that they do more or less the same thing every day at the same time, so that a scout with experience of the habits of animals would very quickly obtain useful information.

Points to remember.

1. It is very important for the scout to learn how to report accurately what he sees and does in as concise a form as possible. It is most difficult in the heat and excitement of battle to sit down and write a clear and legible account of information obtained.

2. The importance of forwarding accurate information was always impressed on all Intelligence Officers, Scout Officers, and men of Intelligence Sections.

3. When undergoing training, scouts should be made to write and forward reports continually until it becomes almost a habit with them to address a report accurately, to give clear, correct and concise information, and to sign correctly.

Landmarks.

Particularly in semi-open or open warfare, he must always note prominent landmarks in the landscape by day and memorize them. Also note marks by night, such as the outlines of trees, hills, contours, trenches, etc.—anything that will help the scout to find his way about both by day and night.

This entails a good eye and memory for country. This is a priceless gift in scouting ; it is born in some, and others acquire it by practical experience. Keen observation and a knowledge of what things to look for is essential.

Finding Camp or your Original Direction without Map or Compass.

In peacetime many a man has been lost by neglecting to take careful note of his surroundings on leaving camp in the morning. Before leaving your camp or trenches or wherever you are, always try to note some landmark near your camp as a reference point ; study this landmark carefully so that you will remember its appearance, then as soon as possible after leaving camp look back and try to pick up some prominent landmark in the distant landscape behind your camp and fix this point in your memory. Keep on looking back and fix the location of your starting-point in reference to these landmarks.

If you cross over an intervening high ridge and descend the other side, you proceed to memorize new landmarks in exactly the same way.

In this manner it is impossible to lose your way in daylight, and an expert scout is equally certain of his direction at night.

There is no more important warning to a scout than to look back and memorize. No matter where he is or what he is doing, he should always take note of prominent features in the landscape.

Forests.

Only safe method is to blaze trees, but this would be dangerous in enemy country.

Trails.

Owing to the stabilized nature of the last war and the hundreds of thousands of men engaged, it was never possible to gain much information from the examination of tracks or trails except from aeroplane photos. Guides were nearly always provided to take platoons in and out of the line during the night. These guides usually reconnoitred this route in daylight if possible. When going into the line with full kit and carrying rations, rifles, etc., men grumbled mightily if guides took them over a bad or extra long route or made them crawl in or out of trenches instead of locating crossing-places over trenches.

Sun.

If the sun can be seen all day, no one should lose his way. Position of sun when setting varies according to time of year and latitude.

Note position of your camp with regard to setting sun, also position of sun when you start out in the morning or afternoon.

Remember whether the sun will have to be in your face or on your back, or on your right or left shoulder, on your way back to camp.

Prevailing Wind.

Remember also that in some countries there is a prevailing wind which blows in a certain direction nearly every day between certain hours. If the direction of this wind is known it will be easy to establish your compass bearing.

Trees.

In some countries trees will give you the direction of North or South. The northern side of the tree is as hard as iron, so hard that it has been known to splinter the blade of an axe, while the southern side is quite soft.

Smoke.

Be careful about smoke. It will give away the enemy's position as well as your own. With scouts or patrols it has been used in past wars as a decoy sometimes. Light a fire, then cache yourself away in a good place for observation, sometimes up a tree, but be careful. During the last war smoke was on certain occasions used to draw the enemy's fire. Dummy trenches were excavated and fires lighted in a few places at daylight to represent smoke from dugouts.

Matches.

On a dark night a lighted match can be seen from 900 yds., a cigarette 300 yds., and in daylight a puff of smoke from either a pipe or a cigarette can be plainly seen from trenches at 200 yds.

Visibility of Men and Objects.

Troops are visible at 2,000 yds., at which distance a mounted man looks like a mere speck.

At 1,200 yds. infantry can be distinguished from cavalry.

At 1,000 yds. a line of men looks like a broad belt.

At 600 yds. the files of a squad can be counted.

At 400 yds. the movements of the arms and legs can be plainly seen.

An object seems nearer when it has a dark background than when it has a light one, and closer to the observer when the air is clear than when it is raining, snowing, foggy, or the atmosphere is filled with smoke.

An object looks farther off when the observer is facing the sun than when he has his back to it.

Sounds.

On a still night sound travels a long way. A man speaking in an ordinary voice can be heard a long way off. This should never be forgotten by scouts. Far too much noise was frequently made by troops leaving the trenches on relief, also they were frequently allowed to light up cigarettes and pipes when too near the front line.

No scout should ever be detailed for reconnaissance if he has a cold in his head or a cough. In the same way, when scouting in open warfare, if you hear the slightest suspicious noise keep as still as death and listen, because the first one to move should be the first one to die as he will give his position away.

Under similar conditions, the hunter frequently gives his position or presence away first to the animal he is hunting ; unless he is an old hand at the game, he has not the same patience as the animal.

Strong Wind.

When there is a strong wind blowing, always try to scout or patrol with it in your face or " up wind." You can hear movements better and can detect any suspicious smells—tobacco, farmyards, cooking, etc. Eyes are better than hearing in wind. It is necessary for the scout to be particularly alert when a strong wind is blowing. It was always stated by our scouts that they could smell " Fritz " fifty yards away.

Ashes.

When scouting in open warfare, it is always well to examine ashes to find out what the fire was kindled for—cooking, warmth, to destroy anything, etc. Notice tracks around the fire.

Food.

Every scout should be a woodsman—able to cook a meal and prepare a camp or bivouac for himself. Always put up the food you are going to take with you when your stomach is empty. If you pack your haversack immediately after you have had a big feed, it is a hundred to one chance you will start out with insufficient supplies.

Swimming.

Scouts should be able to swim, not only to save their own lives, but also the lives of others.

Signals.

It is most important for scouts to understand semaphore, also morse, if possible ; also to arrange signal code among themselves, particularly when doing night work.

Low Ground.

Always keep in low ground ; never go over the skyline if you can work round it—a very common fault among beginners.

First Aid.

Every scout should know something about first aid ; that is to say, not only how to put on a temporary dressing, but also what **not** to do to a man who has received wounds in dangerous places, particularly when shot through stomach or lungs.

When shot through the stomach, no liquid must be given without instructions from Medical Officer.

When shot through the lungs, the man must be kept from all movement if possible in order to avoid hæmorrhage.

When shot through forearm or hand and an artery is severed, the tourniquet should be applied **above** the elbow ; and in a similar manner, if shot through boot or below knee the tourniquet must be applied **above** the knee.

Animals.

Remember that the position and presence of animals is frequently betrayed by the actions of other animals ; also the presence of human beings is often betrayed by actions of animals.

Birds.

It is always well to watch the action of birds when in contact with the enemy ; an unusual flight or excitement among birds or a bird when there is apparently no cause for it. Keep still, listen and watch.

Ravens.

This is particularly noticeable in countries where ravens exist. They should always be watched, as they have the habit of circling in one spot in the air over any movement on the ground.

Movement.

When under observation movement is the most fatal thing of all for both hunter and hunted. It must be reduced to a minimum.

A quick, sudden movement of hands, body or feet is always dangerous.

Walking.

The feet should be as sensitive as hands. Walk from the thigh and not from knee. Toes and ball of foot should come to ground first. It is usually the heel which makes a noise, particularly among sticks or anything likely to crack or creak—stones, etc.

Keep Still.

If a man under certain conditions will only keep as motionless as possible, it is fairly safe to be in full view of the enemy. Also, by keeping perfectly motionless, caribou and other game have been known to feed within a few yards of a hunter. The late Captain F. C. Selous, the well-known African hunter, relates how on one occasion, while sitting motionless on a rock, watching some mountain sheep, a golden eagle almost settled on his head, mistaking Selous evidently for a stump of a tree.

Small Flag in Parapet.

During trench warfare the fluttering of a small flag or piece of rag stuck in the parapet or on the wire was particularly annoying to a good observer because he could not take his eyes from it. It was believed that the Germans used this device in order to distract attention from some other spot nearby.

Objective or Target.

Do not fix all your attention on your objective or target when either hunting or on patrol or scouting. Think always of what you are doing. This is a common fault.

Remember your own movements. Do not get unduly excited at the prospect of a shot. Remember your feet, keep them as flat as possible, and never raise your head quickly or unduly high from the ground.

Carelessness.

Never allow yourself to become careless when scouting. Some men are apt to become careless as they gain confidence in their own ability and take chances rather than go to the trouble of taking every precaution. I once heard a Scout Officer remark : " Oh, So-and-so has cold feet ; he crawls about No Man's Land, whereas I never crawl unless close to the Boche wire." The man who thinks it beneath his dignity to crawl soon becomes a casualty.

Flanks.

Continually watch your flanks when scouting. Nothing is more important ; your eyes must wander carefully everywhere. Danger is nearly always to be feared from behind. When stealth is being used, both men and animals attempt to surprise their prey from behind.

Protective Colour.

The study of colour and background and practical use of these two things is of paramount importance to nearly all arms of the Service.

Protective colour jumped into prominence during the last war, particularly during the last year.

It is marvellous what can be done by a careful study of colour protection, and some very valuable daylight patrols have been successfully accomplished by its use. It requires to be demonstrated before men realize its value.

Particularly is camouflage valuable for scouting and sniping in open and semi-open warfare.

Veils.

There should always be a certain number of veils in the Scouting Section. They are most valuable at times. Gossamer veiling is best. Colours : Black, brown, fawn, slate, yellow or orange. " Issue " brown is a very bad colour for daylight use. The face should be covered when under observation both by day and night.

Outlines.

When under observation by the enemy, a scout must endeavour to conceal all outlines, particularly shoulders ; head-gear, such as caps with distinct outlines, is bad ; elbows and arms should be held close to the sides, legs close together. Cover face and hands. Scouts' suits are useful particularly when snow is on the ground or if grass should be green.

Finally—

Good scouting is a combination of—
>Common sense ;
>Quick thought and action ;
>Practical experience ;
>Sound body ;
>Good nerve.

Extracts from Captured German Documents.

THE VALUE OF SCOUTS AND OBSERVERS FROM THE GERMAN POINT OF VIEW.

The following extracts illustrate the conclusions arrived at by the German G.H.Q. following the surprise attack on 8th August, 1918 :—

(a) Patrols and Scouts.

" Touch with the enemy must be constantly maintained."

" **Smart N.C.O. Patrols.** Mounted men and cyclists."

" Use of compasses will be necessary in the country where view is difficult."

(b) Observation.

" Considerably more must be done to obtain information regarding enemy's intentions by **watching the ground from special O.Ps.,** taking prisoners, listening sets. The closest vigilance is necessary at daybreak."

SNIPING

Introductory.

Sniping is an old art, but came into its own during the last war. Telescopic sights and sniping rifles were used during the American Civil War and in the Indian Mutiny ; also at Bisley in 1900. The earliest British patent is dated January, 1854.

Establishment, 1940.

Eight per battalion under Intelligence Officer. Suggest eight more for replacements.

Definition.

An expert rifleman " out to kill " who is highly trained in observation and the use of ground ; equally valuable in trench and open warfare.

He should be able to pick out targets exposed for only short periods, and kill with a single shot from concealed positions.

Qualifications.

Good eyesight and able to use it. Must not be colour blind.
Must not be deaf.
Keen, cool, courageous, persistent, good shot, truthful, **patient.**
Good scout, good eye for ground, particularly in open warfare, and able to read it quickly.
Highly strung, nervous temperament, restless, not likely to be good.

Must have knowledge of—

1. Causes of inaccuracy in shooting and defects in rifle.

2. Use and care of telescope and telescopic sights.

3. Observation.

4. Construction of concealed hides and loopholes.

5. Map reading.

6. Use of compass.

7. Sketching.

8. Value of protective colour.

9. Scouting and use of ground.

10. Night sniping.

11. Penetrations.

12. Wind.

13. Elevation.

14. Judging distance.

15. Messages and reports.

Selection of Men.

1. Take great care.

2. Good shooting essential, but by no means only qualification.

3. Observant to highest degree.

4. Stalkers, keepers, poachers, prospectors, trappers, out-of-door people, hill and moorland farmers, etc.

It is useless to try to make a sniper out of every man in a battalion. Only a limited number are available, but they must be specialists reserved for sniping.

Demands—

Patience, perseverance and pluck with precision both of the man and his weapon.

Objects of Sniping.

Let us consider first the objects of sniping, then the means by which they may be best attained.

1. To protect your own trenches and F.D.Ls., both in positional and open warfare (front, support, communication trenches, and all approaches). This involves—

    (a) Obtaining a superiority of fire and keeping down that of the enemy.

    (b) Obtaining a mastery over the enemy snipers. Making a thorough visual reconnaissance of the enemy's position and obtaining all useful information.

2. To kill the enemy sniper and shake the enemy's morale—the two objects go hand-in-hand together.

If the enemy is allowed a quiet time he will utilize it for work of attack and defence. A few well-trained snipers can keep him quiet by their determination with accurate fire and produce an effect that is not measured by the number of rounds fired.

It seems to be a prevalent idea in many quarters that a sniper is a species of machine gun whose sole object is to dispose rapidly of large numbers of the enemy. Such an idea is erroneous. The sniper's first value is in defence, to prevent casualties on his own side, and he should never resort to rapid fire except, of course, in dire necessity.

Observation and the ability to describe what he has seen are most important qualifications in a sniper, scout or observer. Good shooting is an essential but by no means the only qualification ; men selected must be observant to the highest degree. The sniper should be able to pick out targets that are not obvious to the ordinary view.

He is out to kill special targets, men who know as much about the game as himself and can make use of—

            Concealment,

            Disguises,

            Protective colour.

This will be impossible of accomplishment unless your sniper is observant and knows what to look for and how to look for it. This requires special training.

Sniping can be of two kinds—Organized and unorganized.

Unorganized Sniping.

Unorganized sniping has proved to be more or less useless. There is no one to guide them, to instruct them, to see that they snipe and not sleep, that they keep the Hun sniper in hand, and that they are taking **an intelligent interest in their work.**

Battalions who have no snipers or unorganized ones are bound to lose men at the hands of German snipers. In some such instances the casualties were very serious.

I know of one particular instance during the last war, in 1916, when a Brigadier of the 121st Infantry Brigade, occupying trenches at Ploegsteert, suffered so many casualties from Hun snipers that he came up to the Second Army Sniping School and asked us if we could do anything for him, so we gave special training to two of his officers and sixteen men and sent them off. Some two weeks later we received a letter from this Brigadier, stating that the sniping had been checked and the tables turned, and that one of the most dangerous and persistent snipers had been spotted by using a camouflaged head, two of which we gave the sniping officer and trained him in their use. The head was carefully exposed and the Hun immediately bit, but missed with his first shot ; the second shot, however, hit the dummy head in the eye and came out behind. By looking through the holes with a periscope the Boche was spotted in a tree and killed.

That is an instance of unorganized sniping and its effect, and then of organized sniping and its effect.

Organized Sniping.

This depends on—

The General Situation.—That is to say, what opportunities are afforded for sniping in the front and support lines or in front of the line and so on. How you will use your snipers. Where you will place them.

Enemy Activity.—Whether he is very aggressive and his sniping good and he has many sniping positions and has good command of our lines.

Nature of Front.—Whether lines are close or far apart. If very close sniperscopes will probably be the only available method, unless we at the same time have sniping positions behind on high ground. If both conditions exist more snipers will be required.

Ground.

Snipers must also have a good eye for ground and be able to read it quickly, and know how to make a successful stalk, should such an opportunity occur. This is a very important part of a sniper's training. They cannot have too much of it, whether they are operating in trench warfare or open warfare.

Great stress should be laid on watching the actions of animals and birds at all times, and noting how frequently the position of human beings is given away by the actions of animals, etc. Also protective colour is not sufficiently understood by snipers, scouts and observers.

In position warfare we are very much like animals. We do the same thing more or less in the same way day after day. Therefore a knowledge of the habits of animals is quite an asset to begin with.

23

Outlines.

Snipers must know how dangerous outlines are : head and tin hat, elbow, shoulders, field-glasses, arm from side, legs open, etc.

Be careful when stalking an enemy that you are not yourself being stalked.

Watch flanks at all times. Expect danger from every side and not only from your front.

Movement.

Particularly quick movement is a most fatal thing to both hunter and hunted, and must be reduced to a minimum. A quick, sudden movement of hands, body or feet is very noticeable.

The flutterings of a small piece of rag on a stick or a piece of sandbag on wire will attract the observer's attention immediately. The same thing applies to movement of hands, head and feet when under observation.

When sniping from shell holes or other places in No Man's Land, the sniper is far more likely to give his position away by movement than by fire.

Protective Colour.

The author is a very great believer in protective colour and disguises for both observers and snipers. To use them properly, however, much experience and practice are required.

A great many men fail to appreciate what can be done until it has been demonstrated to them.

The amount of camouflage material which is being used and which has been used in this war is something astounding : millions of yards of chicken netting tied with dummy grass ; painted canvas, also in millions of yards ; dummy trees, dummy men, dummy loopholes.

Protective colour is priceless for daylight sniping or patrol work or stationary daylight observation close up to Boche lines.

Tasks of Snipers.

1. Keep down enemy morale.

2. Special targets : enemy commanders, N.C.Os., anyone directing operations, working parties, artillery F.O.Os., etc., machine guns.

3. Protect forward defended localities.

4. Enemy snipers.

5. Preparation of hides and loopholes.

General.

1. In the open snipers will generally work alone ; in permanent loopholes with observer, if possible.

2. Must not fire rapid from concealed positions.

3. Best rifle and sight : P.14 and P.18, 1940.

4. Zeroing : Whenever possible before sniping. Use any means— i.e., tin can, etc.

5. Report sniping casualties so that cause can be investigated.

6. Movement in concealed positions is worse than fire from them.

7. In damp and mist, discharge of rifle is easily seen. In very hot weather also dust.

8. Best sniping range is up to 300 yds. from target, not more.

Summary.

" The art of the hunter coupled with the wiles of the poacher and the skill of the target expert armed with the best aids that science can produce."

Good Shooting.

During the Second Battle of Ypres, over 200 deliberate shots were fired at close range at advancing Germans by a King's Prizewinner. He must have accounted for nearly 150 casualties.

The following is from the records of the last war :—

CANADIAN CORPS,
I.G. 864,

19th May, 1917.

CANADIAN CORPS TRAINING SCHOOL.

HITS CLAIMED BY SNIPERS FROM DIVISIONAL SUMMARIES.

Period : January 1st—April 5th.

1st Canadian Division ...	48
2nd Canadian Division	96
3rd Canadian Division	262
Total	406

During the same period prisoners captured by this Corps stated that twenty-six men had been killed by direct hits in the head by our snipers. As prisoners were not captured belonging to each company of the various battalions and regiments in the line from January to April, it was impossible to check the figures given by the divisions. All prisoners captured, however, stated that the accuracy of our snipers was marvellous, and much respected.

Two cases are worthy of note—

(a) Prisoner stated that in a fourteen-day tour ten men were killed.

(b) Prisoner stated that in a five-day tour seven men were killed.

Assuming that a German company held a line of 400 yds. and the Canadian Corps held a line of 20,000 yds., approximately fifty German companies would be necessary to hold the line opposite to us, and if the average referred to by prisoners of one killed per company per day held good for the Corps front, it seems fifty Germans were killed per day, and a complete German battalion wiped out in twenty days.

Night Sniping.

This can be carried out with great success if men are carefully selected and trained.

Brave but excitable men are useless for this work.

Snipers must know the ground thoroughly and have fixed boundaries.

Machine guns should be warned that our snipers are out.

Snipers should use telescopic sights. Range up to 200 yds. on darkish night.

Best time : summer evenings or moonlight nights.

Snipers must be careful in selection of ammunition for night sniping, always using a brand they know. (Test behind lines.)

No oil in bore of rifle on any account. Work bolt slowly.

Keep low ; never stand upright within 100 yds. of enemy's trench.

Also keep in low ground and avoid skyline.

Fog.

Sniping in fog is good ; it is possible to get a better sight than at night. Always aim low in fog.

Stalking.

It is frequently possible at night to spot sentries on trench duty where heads appear at intervals over the top of the parapet or out of a sap. The sniper should take advantage of such exposures.

When consolidation of a new line is taking place, working parties will be active at night and the night sniper will secure many targets.

Very lights or flares are fired at intervals from trenches or shell holes. In performing the act the firer will frequently be seen and should be stalked.

Sniperscopes.

These should always be used when front-line trenches are close together, or amongst mine craters when the lips are occupied one side by us and the other by the enemy. Very accurate shooting can be done with sniperscopes. The definition of the sights is much clearer, and it is not necessary to employ crack shots. Also personal error is to a large extent eliminated.

Four-inch groups at 100 yds. can be obtained by anyone who knows anything about shooting after a little practice. Wherever possible the rifle should be concealed on the parapet and should have an oblique line of sight ; the sniperscope should be disguised with sandbagging. Always aim low with sniperscopes.

It is only necessary to occupy trenches dominated by Boche snipers to know what a bad moral effect such sniping has on everyone, and how pleasant it is when we can again walk about without danger of being sniped.

Authentic Records of Snipers in Open Warfare.

" At Valenciennes on the Canal de l'Escaut between October 24th and 29th more targets were exposed and more hits registered than would probably have been the case in six months of trench warfare."

It is considered that a citation of the deeds performed by some Canadian snipers during the last hundred days of the war will help not only to illustrate but imprint on the minds of students the value of expert shooting coupled with pluck and endurance.

1. " At Cagnicourt, September 2nd, 1918, snipers worked forward to the flanks of isolated machine guns, also field artillery which was firing over open sights, and successfully put them out of action."

2. " On August 9th, 1918, at Vrely the 25th Battalion was held up by machine-gun fire, and there was not sufficient cover for Lewis-gun crews to work forward. The battalion snipers worked forward and, getting round the enemy's machine-gun positions, forced them to be vacated."

3. " At Meharicourt on August 9th the 22nd Battalion carried out the consolidation of the line reached by them under cover of the fire of their snipers."

4. " On September 9th at Vis-en-Artois two enemy snipers caused a great many casualties ; ten officers and runners of the 18th Battalion who were endeavouring to obtain information as to line reached and the dispositions of the battalion.

" The consequent lack of information prevented the battalion from renewing attack for a considerable time."

5. " During the advance on Cambrai two 2nd C.M.R. battalion snipers took up a position, located a field gun firing point blank at the advancing infantry, and shot the two gunners, thus putting the gun out of action."

6. " In the battle east of Arras on 26th August, 1918, the advance of the 4th C.M.R. Battalion was held up by strong enemy machine-gun fire. Three snipers went out to the flank and picked off the crews of four machine guns. They then rushed the post, capturing the four guns and fourteen prisoners."

7. " At Le Quesnel on August 9th one Boche sniper did more damage than four machine guns which were firing from the same locality. The guns were located, the sniper was not."

8. " During the advance through the Forêt-de-Raismes our snipers were continuously engaged with rearguard snipers of the enemy, driving them from their positions and by using initiative and pluck they enabled the battalion to advance on one day more than six kilometres with only a few casualties in the Scout Section and one in the companies."

9. " On August 8th, 1918, in the vicinity of Folies, a German officer could be seen in a trench commanding a number of men and personally directing the fire of two machine-guns which in turn were holding up our advance.

" A sniper shot and killed the officer, with the result that in a short time both the machine guns were captured, together with about forty men."

SNIPING FROM HOUSES, BUILDINGS, BEHIND WALLS, ETC.

During open warfare snipers must be prepared to take advantage of any position which may help to inflict casualties on the enemy and open the way for the advance of our soldiers, not only in open country when enemy machine guns are holding them up, but also in villages—outlying buildings, rooms in houses, cellars, walls, chimney-pots, and through the roofs of houses which have been partly demolished by shell fire, etc.

Rooms in Isolated Houses or in Streets.

Whether sniping from rooms in isolated houses or houses situated in streets, it is not advisable for the snipers to occupy rooms on the ground floor. These can be mopped up systematically and quickly by our own infantry. Until the advance troops arrive, snipers should go forward and attempt to establish themselves in the nearest house or houses, preferably in the second storey. If they occupy ground-floor rooms they will present an easy target to the enemy provided with hand grenades. Our snipers should carry at least two grenades for their own protection and to clear enemy snipers out of rooms if they are unable to do so by rifle fire. These grenades may also be of much service should our sniper have been discovered and an attempt made in force to kill or capture him.

Rooms—out of Windows—Second Storey.

Select, if possible, rooms in the second storey. In most cases all glass will be shattered from the windows and only frames left. Window space may be wide open and no frames left. In any case the sniper must never expose his head or any part of his body out of the window for the purpose of sniping. He should take up a position in the room which will give him an oblique line of fire protected by the wall of the room and well clear of the window. If unable to get good view while standing on the floor of the room, the sniper can pull out a bed or chair or table, and for protection may possibly use mattresses, pillows, furniture, etc.

Removing Bricks.

If it is possible to do so the sniper may remove a few bricks in the wall for loophole purposes. These should be in the lower part of the wall so that the aperture may be fired through either in a prone or kneeling position.

Line of Retreat.

When occupying a room of this description the sniper should not overlook his possible line of retreat in the event of being spotted and finding it necessary to move to another position. Both in occupying the house and leaving it, the sniper must be on the alert, keeping close to the walls, watching carefully any houses on the opposite side of the street, making use of doorways for temporary observation, being careful about his own shadow if in sunshine and turning a corner, when it is best to go down on hands and knees or crawl.

Walls—unless breached by Shell Fire.

Selection of walls remaining after shell fire, or low walls bordering gardens or roads. Unless these have been breached by shell fire, snipers should never fire over the top—unless, of course, the tops of the walls have been knocked about, leaving a very uneven surface so that the sniper, while keeping close to the wall, can fire over the top at an oblique angle, while his head and body are protected from a shot fired at right angles to him.

In most instances it will be found that a prone position on the ground at either end of the wall may give better results. Here the sniper must keep very low and be careful about his steel helmet if wearing one, as the outline will be dangerous.

Roofs of Houses.

When houses have been shelled and portions of the roof knocked in, snipers should climb into the rafters or get behind the remains of brick chimneys passing through the roof and take up a position for sniping ; these form excellent sniping posts.

Chimney-pots.

Our snipers on several occasions in 1918 placed themselves behind rows of chimney-pots, firing between the various chimneys. These were most effective sniping posts and hardly ever spotted.

To Sum Up.

In open warfare small villages and small towns are mopped up in more or less quick time, so that snipers are usually able to move fairly rapidly from one position to another and thereby try to cover the troops who are operating in the streets and among the ground-floor rooms and houses. Snipers should keep a sharp look-out for enemy snipers who may have concealed themselves (very often in cellars) from the first wave of troops passing through villages, and who then emerge and proceed to snipe our men in the back with unpleasant precision, and then surrender themselves when they cannot safely kill any more.

Approach Work.

Sniping from buildings is dangerous work for snipers, not so much the actual firing from buildings but in approach work—in occupying positions. It must be realized that one sniper could cover any movement up a long open street without any turnings in it, and that by two snipers working together, one on either side of the street, severe casualties could be inflicted. It is therefore far better to select an approach by a back door instead of the front—much more cover may usually be found on the premises behind houses than in front. Only the most expert snipers should be detailed for this kind of work.

CARE AND USE OF THE TELESCOPE

General.

1. For concentrated detail the telescope is unrivalled ; it will out-range any field-glass. The telescope can be used at all times for long-range work behind the fighting line, but for front-line work in open warfare field-glasses are best.

2. It is far easier to conceal than binoculars.

3. If you are given a telescope, " Take care ; treat with respect ; don't lend ; best friend "—otherwise useless as observer.

Types of Telescopes Used.

1. Ross No. 4, Large Aperture.—Object glass, $1\frac{3}{4}$ in. Power 20. Draws 3. Closed $10\frac{1}{4}$ in., open $30\frac{1}{2}$ in. Weight 2 lb. 3 oz.

2. Scout Regiments, Mark IIs.—Object glass 2 in. Power 22. Draws 3. Closed $10\frac{1}{2}$ in. Open 30 in. Weight 2 lb. $1\frac{1}{2}$ oz. Sunshade, open, $1\frac{3}{4}$ in.

3. The G.S. Telescope.—Canada balsam not used between lenses of object glass. When a G.S. telescope has been taken to pieces, the only difficulty in assembling it again will be the replacing of the two lenses forming the object glass.

RULES.

1. The convex lens is always next to the object glass and is therefore replaced first.

2. On the side of the lenses forming the object glass an arrow-head will be found cut into the glass. Before the lenses are put back, this arrow-head must be completed and the middle groove of the arrow must be allowed to slide over the barb or raised line in the cell.

Care and Cleaning.

1. The first thing to remember is that the lenses of all telescopes are made of very soft glass and that this glass is polished to a very high degree. A few scratches on the outer surface of the object glass will negative the value of the best telescope. When the telescope is first taken from its case a light film of dust will usually be found to have gathered upon the object glass. This should be flicked off with a hand-kerchief, and if any polishing is necessary it should be done with a piece of chamois leather or well-washed four-by-two. This cleaning material must be free from grit and should therefore be carried in a pocket or pay book, where it will be kept clean. An enormous number of telescopes were ruined during the last war owing to the neglect of this simple precaution.

Special attention should be paid to the cleaning of the object glass, which is very liable to become covered with dust owing to its position and opening and closing of draws.

2. Never on any account touch the glass with finger or thumb.

3. If the glass be allowed to get damp, fogging will result. To cause this fogging to evaporate, remove object glass and eye-piece and lay the telescope out in the sun or in a warm room. Never permit the metal-work to become hotter than the temperature of the hand, otherwise the Canada balsam (which is used to join the concave and convex lenses in the object glass of nearly all high-class telescopes except the G.S.) will melt.

4. If the draws get wet they must be thoroughly dried and slightly lubricated. The same applies to the sun-shade.

5. As a lubricant use french chalk or vaseline ; if the latter, use very lightly and wipe off.

6. Do not bang the telescope about or blacking will chip off inside.

Use.

1. To draw, hold telescope in left hand by the handguard and draw slowly in a circular movement. Close the same way and keep slightly lubricated. After closing, shut eye shutter, replace cap.

N.B.—No concertina method of closing should be permitted.

2. Always extend your sunshade. (More observation posts have been given away by the light shining upon the glass of the telescope than in any other way.) In the last war and the present one we are facing East—therefore need for sunshade particularly in early morning.
When looking into the sun, if necessary use extension to sunshade, brown paper or tin, 9 in. to 1 ft. long. This is a trick borrowed from the chamois hunters in the Alps, and will greatly assist you when looking into the sun.

3. Always mark your focus by scratching a circular ring on the final draw. This will allow you to focus the glass quickly and correctly before putting it to your eye.

4. Always carry slung on body. If you take it off and let it travel in a car or lorry, the jolting will almost certainly ruin it.

5. Always use a rest when observing—*i.e.*, lie down, knees raised and together, support for back of neck, telescope rested along inside knee or on a walking-stick. Must be completely comfortable.

6. Use both eyes alternately to avoid eye-strain.

7. Use with both eyes open.

8. When searching a given sector of ground or trench, divide it into fields of view. Work slowly, allowing fields to overlap.

9. Never neglect suspicious objects. Never leave one without finding out what it is and why it is there.

10. If in doubt, when observing, about some object, look round and round it because the keenest part of one's vision is on the edge of the field of vision, not in the centre of it. It is often said that when you look away for a minute you rest your eyes, and on looking again you can then see better. This is not the case ; it is simply that the field of vision alters and often you see something as you do so. This particularly applies at dawn and dusk.

11. When an object is found, consider—

        (a) Distance,
        (b) Shape,
        (c) Colour,
        (d) Size,
        (e) Position.

12. Remember conditions of visibility are constantly changing. An object which is indistinct at 1100 hrs. may become quite clear at 1105 hrs.—i.e., sunshine and cloud, light and shadow, morning, afternoon and evening.

13. Slight movement is more easily detected if you do not look straight at an object. If you look right, left, above and below you will use the keenest part of your vision.

14. Remember that when there is a heat haze you will often get better results with a low than a high magnification. Conditions in France are more suitable to magnifications of under than over 25. Excellent work can be done in the front line with a glass which magnifies ten times. Use pancratic only for extra special scrutiny of detail.

15. Use detail to check other detail. For instance, if you can pick out the badge on a Hun he will not be more than 200 yds. away.

16. Do not forget that good results can be obtained on clear starlight or moonlight nights by the use of telescopes or night glasses. Generally speaking, the bigger the object glass, the better the results at night.

17. Always be ready to avail yourself of natural conditions. The visibility after a rain shower is almost always good. Snow can be of the greatest assistance to the observer ; it shows up wire and gaps in wire, paths, ground beaten by patrols, etc. The best season for spotting observation posts in the enemy lines is autumn, when the leaves fall and the grass withers.

18. Telescopes should always be disguised by the use of sandbags, or otherwise wrapped about, but great care must be taken that the disguise is not dusty or dirty.

19. Illumination depends on size of object glass. It is absolutely essential as well as magnification, probably more so, especially at night, when a magnification of 10 and good illumination is very effective—one can see things invisible to the naked eye. Strapped on to light machine guns and sighted then for, say, 300 yds., effective shooting can be made.

20. In trench warfare a really good glass man working from the front line by day can make a most valuable wire reconnaissance.

21. Practise picking up movements—*i.e.*, birds, etc.—for quickening. A good shot will probably be a good glass man because he is used to " swing." As a beginner, to practise getting on to objects quickly, once an object is found, look away and then quickly back again.

22. Remember that small near objects are more difficult than distant ones.

For Intelligence Officers.

1. When an officer is inspecting telescopes, he should inspect cases also.

2. Inspection of the telescope (**only** by Intelligence Officers) :—

   (*a*) Push back sunshade and remove object glass. This has two lenses, one concave and one convex, cemented together with Canada balsam.

   (*b*) In replacing object glass, hold telescope, rotate it anti-clockwise. The object glass and lenses must fall by their own weight only. Screw anti-clockwise until the lens " clicks," then screw up clockwise. Very fine thread.

   (*c*) Remove eye-piece—point out shutter.

   (*d*) Remove field lenses ; these are contained in the short barrel which fits into the end of the final draw.

   (*e*) Replace eye-piece as object glass—*i.e.*, anti-clockwise first—then screw up.

The Symien Sniper Suit

The Boiler Sniper Suit

CAMOUFLAGE

INCLUDING METHOD OF USING DUMMY HEAD

Camouflage having played so important a part throughout the war, it is advisable to discuss the art thoroughly.

It is most important that all observers, snipers and scouts, as well as Intelligence Officers, be trained in the possibilities of camouflage—that is to say, " to know what to look for."

Camouflage was brought to a most extraordinary state of efficiency by the British and Germans before the last war ended. The headquarters in France at Wimereux employed many well-known artists and sculptors who produced many useful designs, and made anything from a brick to a full-sized tree, the imitation being so well done that it was impossible to detect the deception except at very close range.

Camouflage may be defined as **deception** or—

(a) " Concealment of the act or fact that something is being concealed."

(b) To render objects indistinguishable or unrecognizable by means of imitation or disguise.

Hiding from view is not by any means the primary aim.

The Ideal.

Perfect camouflage of any work can only be attained by non-interference with the normal or natural aspect of the locality as viewed from the air, and with which the enemy has become familiar. This means—

(a) Very close attention to detail.

(b) Exercise of forethought and imagination.

(c) Preliminary study of aeroplane photographs of the locality to be camouflaged is essential, also the effect of preparatory work.

(d) It is useless to wait until work is accomplished.

Location of Positions.

Positions can be located by—

(a) Aeroplane photography.

(b) Air observation.

(c) Ground observation.

(d) Flash spotting.

(e) Sound ranging.

Aeroplane Photography.

The aeroplane observer is not to be feared nearly so much as the aeroplane photo, together with the man who is able at his leisure to interpret these photographs.

The camera is a most accurate witness, and every effort must be made to defeat the air photograph expert.

A photograph records colours in terms of light and shade and forms a sort of patchwork pattern. The pattern may be large and simple like that on a chess-board, or intricate and confused like that on a painter's palette.

The ideal already defined is more easily attainable when the photograph pattern is complex, and more difficult when the pattern is simple.

It has been stated that the camera reflects light and shade, therefore it is important to have some knowledge of—

(a) What reflects light and shade ;
(b) What absorbs light.

For example—

(a) Billiard table brushed the wrong way.
(b) Top-hat brushed the wrong way.

Grass or vegetation possesses this quality to a marked degree. The longer it is, the darker it is ; but when it has been pressed down, the shadow is lessened and it appears light.

Earth contains little texture, especially if it has been turned up for any length of time and exposed to the sun.

The whole problem, then, is to choose and erect a cover which will reproduce that pattern. This is the basis of successful camouflage.

Concealment.

When planning methods of defeating the camera, it is essential to realize the clues by which any new work is recognized. They are—

1. Disturbance of soil, especially among vegetation.
2. Tracks.
3. Shadows.
4. Regularity.

All these points must be taken into consideration and provided for **beforehand.**

1. Disturbance of Soil.—Among vegetation it is important to conceal all trace of soil from an excavation because it is extremely noticeable. In a locality bare of vegetation it will probably be sufficient to scatter it.

Also preparations for work such as concrete mixing, dumps of stores, etc., should not be exposed to view.

2. Tracks.—Tracks are almost as visible as a searchlight on a dark night. Tracks round an observation post or a battery which has no track discipline act as a signpost to each gun pit or post.

It is nearly impossible to camouflage a much-frequented track if right in the open. Anything opaque enough to hide it would itself cast a shadow. Whatever the locality, the first essential is to confine traffic to one route, which should run as close to natural cover as possible.

[Photo: Mrs. P. Willson.

A good demonstration of Camouflage.

Man leaning against tree, wearing camouflage coat and headpiece.

Camouflaged Sniper lying in grass.

When any work is carried out on grass or in vegetation, an inevitable result is the trampling down of a considerable area all round. This area must all be included in the camouflage. It is impossible to underestimate the importance of concealing tracks.

Many a position which is well concealed in other respects has been given away by tracks.

3. Shadows.—When studying an aeroplane photo the first step is to ascertain the direction of light in order that the form of any excavation or erection may be determined by the shape of the shadows cast, and to differentiate between convex and concave shapes, such as a mound and a shell hole. Therefore in erecting camouflage it must conform to the general shape of the surrounding locality.

A mound must be replaced by a mound and a flat surface by a flat surface.

A concealed trench may be betrayed by the sagging of the camouflage cover, the shadow conforming exactly to the line of the trench.

4. Regularity.—Anything of a rectangular or regular shape arrests the attention when a photograph is examined. Nothing in nature appears regular, consequently anything that is regular must be the work of human hands and therefore receives close inspection.

Regularity is frequently manifested in the regular spacing or dressing of emplacements.

Summary of Principles.

The principles of camouflage can be briefly summarized thus :—

(a) Reproduction of the ground pattern or substitution for it of something that is not unnatural or abnormal.

(b) Adequate concealment of work from the very beginning and of all evidence of occupation.

(c) Deception and not concealment is the object of camouflage.

The only practical method of planning the concealment of any work is to plan it with reference to a recent photograph of the locality.

Use of Camouflage.

1. Colour.—If a net is too green for its surroundings, dead grass will alter the tone.

2. Scrim.—Scrim is canvas with an open mesh, painted one colour only, and should never be used by itself in the open. It must be specially painted.

3. Opacity.—The knots of grass attached to camouflage nets are not sufficiently dense to hide light-coloured objects such as sandbags, trench boards, spoil, etc. Coloured scrim or anything that will darken the tone should be spread over such objects.

Wire Netting Camouflage.

As a general rule, wire-netting camouflage is preferable to fish-netting in normal trench warfare, because it is more durable and, once erected, requires little attention ; its chief disadvantage is its bulk, and for a war of continual movement fish-netting is much better.

Type of Camouflage.

What is called "flat-topped" is the most universally suitable type. Having no sides, it admits of convenient access and free movement. It **must** be flat.

It is arranged by having a number of poles connected to each other by cross bracing wires, the whole guyed back to stout pickets. Twelve feet between poles and a height of six feet is the maximum advisable. The lower it can be kept the better.

It must extend well beyond the work in every direction to protect it from oblique view.

Inflammable.

Camouflage material is very inflammable, particularly with howitzers. Provision should be made for replacing any portion which is likely to be burnt.

Wire-netting is safer than fish-netting.

Maintenance.

Camouflage is a continuous process and must be kept abreast of changing conditions, such as seasons of year, different landscapes, fading leaves and grass, etc.

Rapid Advance.

In a rapid advance in open warfare, advantage can be taken of ruins and broken ground and this camouflaged with battle debris.

Observation Posts.

Good observation is of vital importance, and trouble is well expended on concealing its existence and preserving it from destruction. Even if an observation post is proof against shell fire, it disturbs observation to be continually shelled. I suppose less care was given to the construction and camouflaging of observation posts than anything else, particularly in trench warfare. The common procedure was to build the observation post, then attempt to camouflage it, and then continually enter it in full view of the Boche. In many instances well-worn tracks were made from various directions, all terminating at this one spot.

Concealment of Loopholes.

Loopholes can be made absolutely invisible at twenty yards by using gauze painted to match the external appearance of the observation post. This gauze was used with much success during the latter part of trench warfare, but, of course, is not necessary during a rapid advance in open warfare.

False Work.

It was thought feasible at one time to paint dummy trenches on canvas in such a manner as to deceive the enemy photograph expert, but it was found that the painted shadow remained fixed and did not alter in accordance with the position of the sun.

1. Dummy Pill-boxes.—It is sometimes profitable to erect dummy pill-boxes among real ones. These should be strongly constructed so as not to be too susceptible to damage by shell splinters. Painted canvas backed with wire netting on firm supports is good.

2. Dummy Attacks or " Chinese Attacks."—Silhouette figures made of mill-board and well painted have frequently been employed to draw fire from real attacks. They are employed on one or both flanks and exposed a few minutes before zero hour behind a slight smoke screen.

Machine-Gun Emplacements.

It is most important sometimes to conceal machine-gun emplacements. The small size of these emplacements gives one a very wide scope for successful camouflage.

These emplacements come under close observation from low-flying planes, and there have been occasions when a small amount of camouflage would have avoided the destruction of many guns and lives.

A machine-gun should remain undetected while firing if possible. Grass of various shades (to suit surroundings) tied on fish netting could be obtained at any time and were called machine-gun squares. If required for shell holes or bare earth, painted scrim was used and is a good thing. These machine-gun nets are very portable and weigh but a few pounds.

Protective Colour.

Now we come to the question of camouflage for human beings. Up to the present the discussion has been confined to the disguising of inanimate and stationary objects, but there are occasions when camouflage or a knowledge of protective colour can be most valuable to the scout, sniper and observer in order to disguise or conceal movement.

1. Turkish Army.—Snipers of the Turkish Army during the Gallipoli campaign exhibited great cunning in the use of camouflage, and Australian scouts, snipers and observers gained many useful hints during this campaign which were of much use to them later on when they came to France.

2. Animal Life.—Knowledge of animal life and experience of the woods is a great help to the sniping or scout officer in the use of camouflage. Nearly every animal has been given a certain amount of protective colour which will blend more or less with its surroundings in both light and shadow.

A great many animals and birds appear to have very good knowledge of their visibility, and how to render themselves as inconspicuous as possible. When danger is imminent, most animals will attempt to take advantage of protective backgrounds and by remaining motionless will frequently evade detection. Small animals and some birds usually flatten themselves on a protective floor or background and remain motionless and are most difficult to spot at close range.

3. Outlines.—The use of protective colour in the shape of painted suits and hoods, etc., for scouts, observers and snipers not only enables them to assimilate themselves to the colouring of their surroundings, but the suits destroy the fatal outline of a man's head and shoulders.

4. Duck, etc.—Nearly all web-footed birds when wounded seek shelter in water among branches, etc. An ordinary wild duck when swimming with its head erect is very conspicuous, but when winged or wounded it usually seeks the shelter of a bank or overhanging branches and, flattening its neck out on the water, sneaks along or crouches against protective background, but were the bird to hold its neck erect it would be plainly visible.

The following birds exemplify the value of protective colour : snipe, partridge, woodcock, and grouse.

5. Ptarmigan.—This bird's plumage changes with the season from snow white in the winter to grouse in the summer, so that at all seasons of the year it can find protective background.

6. Arctic Hare.—In a similar manner the Arctic hare is pure white in the winter (with the exception of the tips of its ears) and grey in the summer.

7. Frogs, etc.—Frogs, chameleons and lizards, particularly certain types, form the most striking illustration of natural camouflage.

Finally, lectures on camouflage should, if possible, always be accompanied by a practical demonstration, such as an exhibit of snipers' and scouts' suits, hoods, portable observation posts, disguised sniping plates, machine-gun covers, etc.

Intelligent use must be made of camouflage, otherwise it should be left alone.

EXTRACT FROM OPERATION ORDER BY THE 3RD INFANTRY BRIGADE FOR A DUMMY RAID, JUNE 27th/28th, 1917.

1. Camouflage Figures.

(*a*) These figures will be placed in front of the new Dummy Jumping-off trenches that run approximately 200 yds. in advance of the front line of the Centre Battalion between T.24.a.1.9. and T.17.d.7.6. 17.a.9.2.

(*b*) It is expected that the C.E. will deliver these figures at the Quarry headquarters on the night of 26th/27th.

(*c*) On the night of the 27th/28th a party of 2 Officers, 10 N.C.Os. and 200 O.Rs. from the support Battalion (R.M.R.) will carry these figures and their working apparatus, and install them in the Dummy Trench under the supervision of the C.E. and the party of the Royal Highlanders of Canada detailed to work these figures.

A guard must be placed over these figures and their apparatus as if any part is missing it is impossible to work them.

(*d*) A demonstration of the working of these figures will be given at R.E. Park, Aux Rietz, at 10.00 a.m. to-morrow, at which 1 Officer and 30 O.Rs. Royal Highlanders will be present.

2. Further orders as to the operation will be issued later to all concerned.

3. Please acknowledge receipt.

(sd.)

3rd Canadian Infantry Brigade.

DUMMY RAID

DOWN POSITION

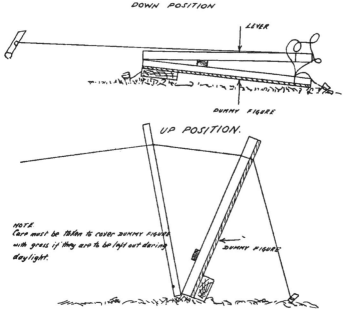

UP POSITION.

NOTE
Care must be taken to cover DUMMY FIGURE with grass if they are to be left out during daylight.

41

SPECIAL WORKS PARK, R.E.
    WIMEREUX.

Reply to your H.O. 698 of June 30th.

The Dummy figures supplied by you proved to be very successful.

They were placed in front of a dummy trench, distant about 600 yds. from the enemy, and were pulled up into a standing position at Zero Hour, under cover of a Smoke Screen.

When the smoke cleared away, the dummy figures and trench were heavily shelled for about 20 minutes.

The method of operating the figures was that suggested and practised by the 46th Division, as follows (see sketch) :—

The figures were fixed to a sill of $2'' \times 6''$ Planking—15 figures on each length of 50 yds. Each length of 50 yds. required two levers to pull the figures to a standing position, wires were attached to these, and run back to our Front Line Trench, 200 yds. in rear. Stop guys must be short enough to prevent the figures coming to a vertical position, so that they will come down again when required.

(*Sd.*)

Major,
General Staff,
1st Canadian Division.

Dummy Header and Stretcher Bags.

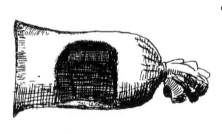

To be used for observation when front-line trenches are very close together and it becomes imperative to keep careful watch on enemy tactics and No Man's Land, etc. When demonstrating these devices to scouts and observers in training they were rarely spotted with the naked eye at so close a range as 10 yds. When in position these dummy bags would appear as in the following diagram.

Gauze Camouflage.

Used as a movable opening for snipers' posts or built into portable and stationary observation posts or for eyepiece in observers' and snipers' hoods.

Snipers' and Observers' Hood.

This is made of prepared sacking (scrim) and camouflaged, and used when looking over the parapet or for use when occupying positions in No Man's Land for daylight observation or sniping.

Common Object Observation Post.

This was called the Common Object Observation Post because the camouflage experts were prepared to duplicate any object whatsoever which might be lying in any advantageous position in or around the front line and which could be turned into an observation post with a little work and careful manipulation. This diagram represents a common entrenching tool which has been lying on the parapet for some time. Both the entrenching tool and a portion of the parapet were reproduced in camouflage, and the real entrenching tool was then removed and the dummy inserted in its place, a narrow excavation was then made from the inner side of the parapet to the entrenching tool and a small observation post established. This was protected as closely as possible by steel sniping plates. The handle of the dummy entrenching tool was made of transparent gauze.

Dummy Header Observation Post.

This is an observation post made of a dummy header bag and was used in the parados in preference to front-line parapet. It was only necessary to push the dummy upwards about two inches to obtain a very extended and clear view of the enemy lines.

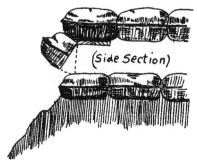

(Side Section)

Parapet Cover, Snipers' Post.

There were many types of light and portable camouflage covers for snipers' plates and observation posts. These two diagrams represent types made for the Vimy front, where few sandbags were used in the parapets.

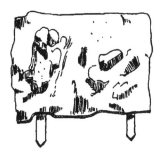 

Periscope disguised in Dummy Header Bag.

This is a simple but most effective disguise for a periscope. If ordinary care is taken in the placing of this bag in the parapet it is almost impossible for any observer to spot the device even at a range of 15 to 20 yds. and using a glass. It should be used whenever possible in all forward saps, bombing posts and places occupied by small garrisons or in any exposed position where keen observation is necessary and care has to be taken not to expose the position of the post. The location of these posts was frequently given away by using naked periscopes.

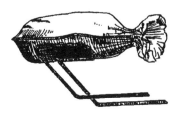

METHOD OF USING DUMMY HEADS.

Dummy Heads.

At Wimereux in France there was established a large camouflage factory under the management of the Royal Engineers and called the Special Works Park, R.Es. At this place dummy heads were cleverly made of papier mâché and moulded from plaster casts taken from employees at the works. These heads were afterwards coloured by well-known artists, some of whom were Royal Academicians.

The special function of these heads was to draw the fire of enemy snipers. On many occasions an aggressive German sniper was so well hidden or protected that our observers were unable to locate him ; it was then that devices had to be thought of which, if successful, would compel him to disclose his position. It was considered that a very life-like representation of a man's head would be more likely than anything else to draw fire, so dummy heads were thought of, made, tested, and gradually sent to Battalion Intelligence Sections on requisition.

Pamphlets describing the methods of exposing heads were sent to all divisions, but very few reached the officers and men who were interested. However, demonstrations were always given at all sniping and scouting schools on the Western Front, so that in time there was at least one officer or man in each Intelligence Section who knew how to manipulate these heads.

Methods.

There were several successful methods used in exposing the dummy heads. In the first place it is essential for the enemy sniper to make a clean hit through any part of the head. A ricochet will not do : it makes too large an aperture to be at all accurate.

The following method was demonstrated practically on a great many occasions and the position of the enemy sniper spotted in less than one minute. This method was greatly facilitated if practised when out in rest billets ; when this is done a tin can is used instead of a dummy head. Two men are required. One man will expose the head very carefully over the parapet ; it should come up gradually and naturally, the head inclining slightly forward and quite vertical. If the head inclines to the right or left or backwards, its nature will be spotted at once. The man holding the head should grasp the " stick " (see Fig. 1), tightly pressing it against the parapet or against a plank standing against the parapet ; this allows the head to be pushed up more smoothly than against sandbags. In some cases the head was operated from a socket or ratchet standing in the trench (see Fig. 2). This method obviates any danger of the head being turned accidentally during exposure or impact of bullet. These stands or ratchets were hardly ever used in the trenches during the war.

With the man holding and exposing the head stands another man, who is armed with a long narrow periscope, and who waits for the enemy sniper to hit the head. If this desired event happens the periscope is held about one foot from the head and the observer lines up the holes as in Fig. 3. If it has been a clean hit and the range not over 250 yds., the enemy sniper will be located with great accuracy.

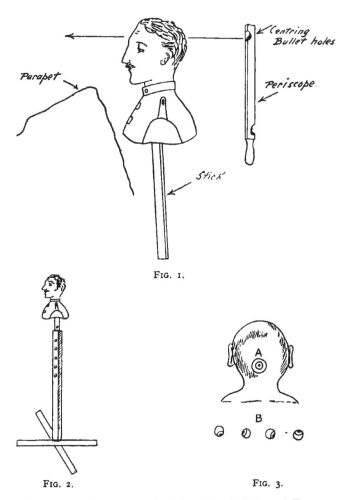

FIG. 1.

FIG. 2.

FIG. 3.

Fig. 3A shows the correct method of centring the holes, and Fig. 3B incorrect methods. The small black spot in centre of the holes in Fig. 3A represents Boche loophole or Boche head, if sniper is in the open.

On one occasion at a range of about 180 yds. a dummy was exposed in the manner described ; it drew fire at once, and the observer, quickly lining up the holes with the periscope, was very grateful to behold the head and shoulders of a German sniper in the act of firing a second shot.

It was thought that if only held in the hands the impact of the bullet would be great enough to knock the head out of alignment, but in practice it was found that the effect of the impact was nil. In some instances it was hardly realized that the head had been hit.

Section VI

THE NEW MILITARY LANDSCAPE SKETCHING

This system of sketching was " invented " by Lieut. W. C. Newton, of the Artists Rifles, and was taught by some of the Army Sniping Schools during the last war, being enthusiastically received.

Landscape (Old Method).

To teach sketching in the old way would require at least two months' constant practice, and even then, unless the pupil had a certain aptitude for the work, it would mean two months wasted.

It was soon realized that in the stormy times of war, when casualties are heavy, some simpler method of teaching sketching must be devised ; hence we have the **Newton Method,** enabling a large percentage of officers, N.C.Os. and men to become fairly expert artists after a few hours' practice.

Bushy Tree		Poplar	
Two Poplars		Willow	
Trees		Shrubs	
Hedge		Church	
Telegraph		Windmill	
Stacks		Trees (in Winter)	
House		River or Stream	
Embankment		Water	

First of all, it is necessary to have a certain number of **Conventional Signs.** Now, these conventional signs will vary according to the country you are in.

Landscapes are very much the same—trees, stacks, windmills, church steeples and undulating country. Therefore we will draw some conventional signs. These signs would be applicable in nearly any part of Europe under war conditions.

Instructions.

Try to do a clear sketch from the start.

Do not expect to have time to polish it up afterwards.

In the field opportunities to redraw sketches are limited.

When drawing

Press on the paper.

Start sharply and finish sharply.

Every line should be put in to express something.

A wavering line which dies away carries no conviction or information because it is the product of a wavering mind.

Definition of Sketch.

Every military sketch has a definite purpose ; it is to give information.

A sketch is a form of report—it is graphic information.

For information clearness is essential, and clearness is attained by two avenues—
  (1) Thought,
  (2) Draughtsmanship ;
and of these the more important is Thought.

Thought.

The form of thought required is a power of simplifying, of analysis. The problem is to direct attention by means of the sketch to some particular point or portion of the landscape, to underline it as it were. But a landscape is a mass of things—crops and grass, hills and trees, houses and valleys, rivers and ruins. It is therefore necessary to analyse the landscape to bring order out of chaos. For this purpose there are three main methods of analysis—
  (a) Separation of planes.
  (b) Encircling or framing-in.
  (c) Division of a whole into parts.
These three methods are neither independent of each other nor yet wholly interdependent. Sometimes all three will be used in the same drawing ; sometimes one will be enough.

It is a question, as will be seen, of the object of the sketch and the nature of the piece of country, and is in all cases a matter of individual judgment and choice.

Before carrying on with the separation of planes, I will give you a few points to remember.

Outlines.

This is purely outline work ; you must not forget this. Draw silhouette of trees, houses and everything else ; it simplifies drawing and things are more easily recognizable by their outlines, which hardly ever change.

The less skilful you are, the more detail you should omit.

Foreground.

Hardly ever to be put in because there is a tendency sometimes to try and identify objects at a distance by objects near at hand. This leads to confusion sometimes, as the sketch may not be used from the exact position where it was made.

Also, it is hard for beginners to draw perspective correctly.

Contrast.

It is sometimes necessary to draw attention to a particular point in the same way as in letter writing we underline certain words for emphasis.

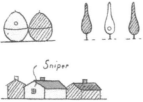

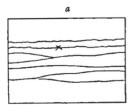

Roads.

It is not advisable for beginners to show roads unless imperative ; it is difficult to draw them to perspective.

Now return to **Separation of Planes.** It is desired to call attention to the point X, and quickly. To save time is always important.

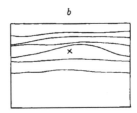

It is plainly a help to the eye to know roughly what sort of distance to expect the object to be.

This can be indicated by drawing the planes. Note the difference between the apparent positions of X in the Figs. *a* and *b*. For this analysis we reduce the piece of country as far as possible to something like the scenery of an outdoor exhibition, the ridges and hills and trees cut out of wood, so to speak, and laid the one behind the other.

The sharp line where a field ends against a copse, the silhouette of trees or houses, the edge where flat land begins to rise—all these will help the analysis into planes.

But it is in each case a matter of choice which to choose and which to omit. It must depend on the purpose of the sketch.

To Sum Up.

Plane analysis is a dividing up of a complex field by means of a series of horizontal but not straight lines **corresponding to recognizable lines on the actual landscape.**

The field of vision is split up into compartments and the possibility of error lessened.

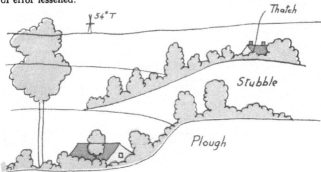

Landmarks or Indication Points.

Prominent landmarks or, as we call them, " Indication Points " are used to draw the observer's attention quickly to the desired spot. Surveyors call the same things " Bearing Trees."

Always draw the horizon first of all and work downwards.

SKETCH SHOWING SNIPERS' POSITIONS, ETC.

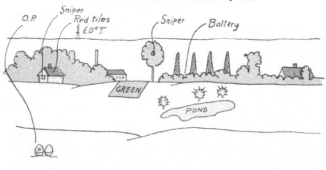

Position :
    60 yds. W. of X Roads,
        Looking North.

NEVILL A. D. ARMSTRONG, *Capt.*,
    16*th Bn. Can. Inf.*,
    Weather—Clear   30 Dec. 16.

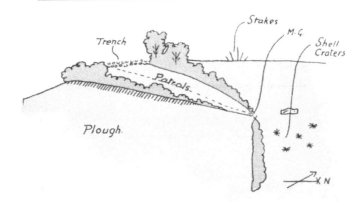

Compass Bearing.

If there should be any prominent landmark on the skyline it might help if one took a bearing to it, but it is not advisable to depend on this for direction on account of mist or fog obscuring the view.

Finishing Off.

On top : title or purpose of sketch. This is the first thing to look for.

Position.—Your own position in lower left-hand corner, stating also direction you were looking when sketching.

In lower right-hand corner—

> Name,
> Weather,
> Date.

Open Warfare.

It is most important in any open warfare, when maps may become scarce or useless, to denote positions of forward troops, etc., *vide* the Somme offensive.

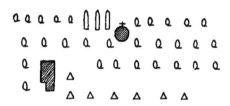

Same Picture.

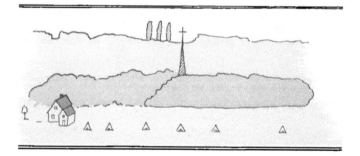

MESSAGES AND REPORTS

MESSAGES.

How to Write.
Message writing.
Abbreviations.
Reconnaissance Reports.
Route Reports.
Patrol Reports.

General.
1. 1 Div.—2 R.W.K.

2. 2 Div. less 2 Bdes.

3. Place names
Personal names
Code names   } in BLOCK CAPITALS.
Regimental names
NOT

4. Do not use " Dawn," " dusk," " may," " should " ; don't be vague.

5. Time and place of arrival of troops : Head of main body.

Date.
1. 2 Feb. 40, **not** 2.2.40 ; first three letters of month. On AFC 2128 day of month only.—*sic.* 2.

2. Night 29/30 Sep.

Time.
1. 0014 hrs., but only 0014 on AFC 2128.

2. Zero plus and minus.

Place.
1. Never give position of H.Q. to which or from which messages sent.

2. Names of places BLOCK CAPITALS.

3. If map reference used, put map sheet in message unless quite clear without.

4. Points described :—
    (*a*) X-roads ½ mile S.E. of BUCKDEN.
    (*b*)   ,,   225° from TRING Church. (On Gridded Maps **Grid**—otherwise **True** bearing.)
    (*c*)   ,,   ½ mile S.E. of **E** in HELBY, **not** *of* Helby.
    (*d*) By co-ordinates, longer.

5. North, South, East, West, but N.W., S.E.
    e.g., South of HEMP, **not** S. of HEMP.
          S.E. ,,   ,,   **not** South-East of HEMP.

6. Road : YORK—RIPON. Railways ditto (capitals).

7. Area : Northernmost first, then clockwise.
   Positions : R. and L. looking towards enemy.

8. Boundaries : Rear to front in advance.
   Front to rear in defence or withdrawal.
   Boundaries between units : Incl. and excl. before place to which
   they refer.

9. Rivers : R. and L. facing downstream.

10. Retirement : R. and L. of own troops ; original R. and L. facing
enemy.

11. Bearings : On gridded map, Grid ; otherwise True.

Hints on Message Writing.

1. Brevity, clearness, observance of rules essential because W/T
must be ciphered.

2. Originator keeps copy.

3. Nothing written above TO on AFC 2128.

4. Names and appointments never shown : TO......... FROM......

5. (a) LUDO—SAGO—BONO : signalled as written to all addressees
       when sender wants each recipient to know to whom
       messages sent.
   (b) LUDO—SAGO—rptd. BONO = LUDO—SAGO for action,
       BONO for information.
   (c) All informed. At end of text. To avoid addressees informing
       each other.

6. Text : Distinguishing letter and number. Letters up to three
unless already allotted.

7. Numbers up to 9999.

8. In text :—
   (a) Word, letter, figure.
   (b) Abbreviated word.
   (c) Combination of letters or figures meaning one
       thing.
   (d) Cipher group to five letters or figures.
   (e) Sign of full stop ⊙

   } One space each.

9. Roman numerals and mathematical signs written in words.

10. Letters, letter ciphers, and important words BLOCK CAPITALS,
otherwise plain hand. Avoid underlinings and oblique strokes.

11. Full stop thus ⊙, in a space to itself. Not necessary at end of
message.

12. ACK or ALL ACK at end of message.

13. Signature : name and rank only.

14. Sign in appropriate space.

15. Degree of priority : Immediate, Important, or leave blank.

16. Time : 24 hr. clock (omit hrs.).

REPORTS.

There are a few fundamental principles to be adopted when reporting. Three of the most essential things in forwarding intelligence are:—

> (1) Accuracy.
> (2) Speed.
> (3) Conciseness.

1. Accuracy.

This can only be attained if the observer or scout has been to some extent trained and knows what to look for and how to report it. Accuracy is of particular importance because if reports have to be verified valuable time is lost.

Beginners should report only what is actually seen or heard. It is sometimes dangerous to attempt to try to draw conclusions from what one sees and hears. In some instances our conclusions may be correct, but in many cases we may be entirely wrong.

2. Speed.

It is of the greatest importance that information should be sent on at once.

It is of little use knowing where the enemy was the day before yesterday if we cannot tell where he is to-day.

A great many men sit on their reports and are afraid to send them in. They continually re-read them and make alterations, etc., and hang on to them hour after hour until whatever value they may have had originally is lost by delay.

3. Conciseness.

> (a) Confine your reports to what is relevant,
>
> (b) Be brief where necessary,
>
> (c) Clear in expression,
>
> (d) And to the point.

Negative Information.

Sometimes of great value, especially to know that the enemy was not in certain places at certain times.

Reports are of three kinds—

> (1) Verbal.
> (2) Written.
> (3) Drawn.

Sometimes a report is a combination of all three.

1. Verbal.

A verbal report is one made by word of mouth.

> (a) Do not speak in a hurry.
>
> (b) Before you begin, make up your mind exactly what you are going to say and repeat it to yourself. On the other hand, when you send a verbal message, have it repeated to you.

F
57

2. Written.

A written report is always preferable to a verbal one, no matter how dirty or untidy the paper may be upon which it is written.

- (a) Write as clearly as possible, and always with the names of places in capital letters (BLOCK CAPITALS).
- (b) Always read over what you have written in order to check mistakes.
- (c) Always state the place from which your report is sent, also do not omit date and time.
- (d) It is important in sniping and intelligence to keep a copy of all reports you make.
- (e) Vagueness: Avoid vague and indefinite terms, such as " dawn," " dusk," " behind," " beyond," " on this side of."

3. Drawn.

Without a sketch it is sometimes impossible to explain a report.

Deductions from Information.

1. In forwarding information from the front line, careful deductions must be made from **facts,** not facts postulated from **deductions.**

2. You must not jump to conclusions. Always state how information was acquired and try to confirm it from every available source.

3. Old information is of no value.

4. Accuracy of details is most important.

5. The nearer the front line, the more reliable is the information.

A few further Hints on Reports.

1. **Time Clock.**—24 hour.

NOON TO MIDNIGHT   MIDNIGHT TO NOON

NOON is written 1200 hrs. noon; MIDNIGHT 2400 hrs. 2nd/3rd Oct.

2. **Bearings.**—It is generally understood that all bearings should be True Bearings unless otherwise stated; but during the period of trench warfare and the use of squared maps, all bearings given were Grid Bearings when a minus difference of some 2° 30′ occurred over a True North Bearing.

3. **River Banks.**—In referring to river banks, it is always supposed that one faces downstream, right-hand being right bank, and left-hand left bank.

58

4. Open Warfare.—Before starting to collect information, understand exactly what information is wanted and concentrate on this work alone ; do not allow yourself to be delayed by interesting but possibly unimportant events, which continually crop up during an attack and a successful advance.

5. Capacity of Roads.

> 9 feet in width, allow transit of infantry in 3's.
> 15 feet in width, allow transit of cavalry in sections (4 abreast).
> 18 feet in width (double traffic), allow transit of guns and waggons.

6. Roads.—It should be remembered that military traffic is very severe on roads. A special note should be made of any very bad portions of a road.

7. Gradients.—As a rule only steep gradients are reported ; the length of these should be given.

8. Surrounding Country.—When reporting on new or conquered country for purposes of defence or further advance, very much detail can, of course, be given ; but generally speaking, and if time for the report is short, it is advisable to state—

(a) If the country is open or intersected by hedges, ditches, etc.

(b) General conditions prevailing.

(c) If there are any parallel roads or small roads branching off, etc.

9. Rivers, Streams, Canals.—Report the general character, such as width, depth, velocity ; nature of banks and points for crossing ; watering-places for horses ; bridges, etc.

10. Woods, etc.—Take note of—

> Size of wood.
> Kind of trees.
> Can guns or cavalry pass through ?
> If there is much undergrowth.
> Any roads or footpaths.
> If it is too thick for the passage of any troops.

11. Troops reported as reaching a Certain Place at a Certain Time.

(a) It is always assumed that the head of the main body is meant unless otherwise stated.

(b) When issuing orders to scouts, always state the place to which reports are to be sent. Usually the Report Centre.

(c) Never use the words " from " or " to " without saying " inclusive " or " exclusive."

(d) All reports must be signed ; this precaution is frequently omitted through carelessness.

(e) In case of a private give number, rank, name, regiment, date and time. Officer : Name, rank, regiment, date, place.
And when sending back information during an attack, always state Platoon and Company.

MAP READING

(Required : 1-inch Maps.)

INTRODUCTORY—CONVENTIONAL SIGNS AND CO-ORDINATES

The expression " Map Reading " is a correct one, as we must be able to read a map in the same way as we read a newspaper.

The ground is made up of direction (or distance) and altitude, and it is therefore the duty of the map to represent that height and distance. As the map is a flat piece of paper, altitude has to be represented by artificial means. This is done by contours.

All maps are inaccurate in some respects. They are a compromise between actual fact and what it is possible to put on paper. As in all compromises, something has to be sacrificed, and here the chief difficulty is that of representing a curved surface on a flat one.

Projection.

Maps are projected—*i.e.*, drawn—by Mercator's Projection or by the Polyconic system.

Kinds.

There are three kinds of maps—

(1) Atlas.
(2) Topographical.
(3) Cadastral.

Atlas.—Describes countries and continents and is on a very small scale—*i.e.*, seldom bigger than 1/100,000 down to 1/1,000,000, 1/M. Only main features shown.

Topographical.—Show topographical features, such as hills, valleys, streams, slopes, etc. Moderate scale, 1/100,000 up to 1 in. as in motor maps.

Cadastral.—For purposes of taxation, showing areas and boundaries of properties. Scale 1/20,000 upwards to 6 in. As maps become larger, they become more like plans than maps, hence cadastral maps are often called plans.

A map should answer four questions—

(1) Which way ?
(2) How far ?
(3) What type of country ?
(4) Where am I ?

These questions are answered (*a*) by conventional signs, and (*b*) by devices which show slopes and scales.

Regarding conventional signs, all necessary information is given at the bottom of the map. This should enable you to understand perfectly everything on the map. There are various types of conventional signs, and it is obviously impossible to learn them all at once.

Regarding map references, first you must understand this diagram.

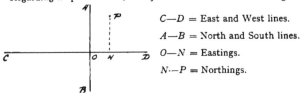

C—D = East and West lines.

A—B = North and South lines.

O—N = Eastings.

N·—P = Northings.

If position of O is known and fixed, it may be used as a point of reference.

RULE.—(1) Eastings first, Northings second.
(2) Same number of figures given in each case and whole reference an even number of figures, 4 or 6.

CONTOURS, GRADIENTS AND MUTUAL VISIBILITY.

Contours are by far the most difficult part of map reading, and a proper understanding of them is the basis of successful military map reading.

As already mentioned a map should answer four questions:—

(1) Which way ?
(2) How far ?
(3) What type of country ?
(4) Where am I ?

To answer the third question it is necessary to understand contours.

Now there are various ways of showing hill features on maps :

(1) By shading,
(2) By hachures,
(3) By layer tints,
(4) By spot heights,
(5) By contours.

Contours are the only sound method for military purposes. Shading is rarely found except in conjunction with hachuring and contours. You will seldom find hachures and contours on the same map.

(Hachures have this great disadvantage : On a map of a fairly flat piece of country they will have to be used to show the smallest rise in the ground. However, in a map of mountainous country, the same degree of hachure may be representing a big precipice. This makes proper comparison between maps extremely difficult.)

Layer tints are invariably used with contours.

Spot heights will be found on practically every map.

Description.

Contours are of vital importance from a military point of view, as from them the soldier can gather from the map where dead ground lies, what point is visible from another, and the gradient of any slope in its relation to manœuvre and transportation.

A contour is simply this : " An imaginary line passing through a series of points each the same height above sea level."

Imagine, then, if you like, as a shore, lines showing successive inundations, with the bays and headlands equalling valleys and spurs.

Take a model of 1/12—*i.e.*, 1 in. to a foot. The model would look like this.

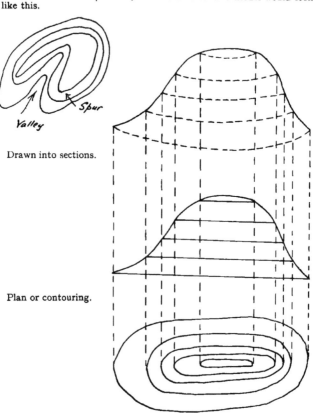

Valley

Spur

Drawn into sections.

Plan or contouring.

Contours can portray any of the following :—

(1) An island.
(2) A valley.
(3) Concave or convex slopes.
(4) A ridge.
(5) A peak.
(6) A spur.
(7) A re-entrant saddle.
(8) A plateau.
(9) A steep slope.
(10) An easy slope.
(11) A knoll.
(12) A cliff or scarp.
(13) A gorge.

Expert map readers will seldom look at contour lines or spot heights when consulting a map. The first thing that they will study is the general run of the water-courses, rivers, lakes, ponds, etc. For where they exist there will be valleys, and on either side of them will be high ground.

Here are three definite rules as to contouring which, if followed, will solve most contouring problems :—

(1) When contours are evenly spaced, the slope is uniform. (Close spacing indicates a steep slope, wide spacing a gentle slope.)

(2) When the spacing reading from high to low decreases, the slope is convex.

(3) When the spacing reading from high to low increases, the slope is concave.

NOTE.—Convex slopes imply dead ground.

Mutual Visibility.

On 1-in. maps the vertical interval, commonly known as the V.I., is usually 50 ft. ; that is to say, the difference in height between contour lines is 50, and therefore features of real tactical importance (but less than 50 ft.) may not be shown. Therefore, though a hill on a 1-in. map may be concave, the top and bottom (points A and B) may not be mutually visible. This is the limitation of a contoured map.

Mutual visibility is of vital importance to you, for upon it are dependent fixed lines, fields of fire from loopholes, and what you can see from an observation post.

METHOD A : SECTIONING.—Take a piece of contouring at random. Draw parallel lines (the same number as there are contour lines in the piece of contouring). Then draw a vertical scale as illustrated below.

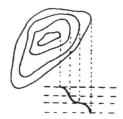

Vertical Intervals.

NOTE.—The horizontal scale should be about six times less than the vertical.

        Join 0 to   0
              50 to 50
              100 to 100 at the intersecting points.

This will present a fairly accurate representation of the slopes, and from this you will see whether any points on that hill are mutually visible.

Gradients.

Gradients are an important part of map reading, in so far as they show the rise or fall of a hill or road over a given distance ; also in their relation to mutual visibility.

If an armoured vehicle can only climb gradients of less than 1 in 6, it cannot go up a road of 1 in 4. This demonstrates the importance of being able to work out a gradient.

A gradient of 1 in 6 means this : In 6 ft. a hill (or road) rises 1 ft. —6 ft. along the floor, 1 ft. up the wall.

        1 is the vertical interval   ...   .   V.I.
        6 is the horizontal equivalent   ...   ...   H.E.

NOTE.—The V.I. is usually in feet, the H.E. in yards.

Take a contour on the map. Measure the distance between the two contour lines, e.g. 150 yds. (i.e., the H.E.). Find out the V.I., e.g. 50 ft. The gradient is $\frac{50}{450} = \frac{1}{9}$.

Therefore the road is passable, as 1 in 9 is less steep than 1 in 6.

Length of slope can only be measured with clinometer or sights which measure angles. One degree subtends 1 ft. in 60 ft.

Visibility.

We have previously said how mutual visibility can be worked out by sectioning.

We have also seen how in concave slopes the top and bottom of the slopes are usually inter-visible, and in convex slopes usually invisible. The best method of testing mutual visibility is by gradients.

Take three points on a hill, A, B and C.

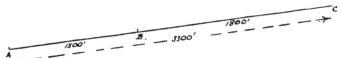

Heights : AB 30 ft., AC 50 ft.

$$AC \quad \frac{50}{3300} \quad = \quad \frac{1}{66} \qquad\qquad AB \quad \frac{30}{1500} \quad = \quad \frac{1}{50}$$

Therefore AB is steeper than AC, so A and C are NOT mutually visible.

By proportion :

$$1500 : 3300 :: x : 50$$
$$x = \frac{1500 \times 50}{3300}$$
$$= 22 \cdot 7.$$

Therefore line of sight at 1500 rises 22·7, but height at B is 30 ft.

Therefore A and C are NOT mutually visible.

A more common problem is when A, D, E are three different hills ; height, for example, 303, 353 and 378 ft. This, worked out by proportion, is :

	Difference in height—
A—D, 700 yds.	A—D, 50 ft.
A—E, 1520 yds.	A—E, 75 ft.

The line of sight from A to E rises 75 ft. in 1520 yds.   The amount it will rise in 700 yds. is found by proportion as follows :—

$$700 : 1520 :: x : 75$$
$$x = \frac{700 \times 75}{1520} = 34 \cdot 5 \text{ ft.}$$

Therefore the line of sight at 700 yds. will rise 34·5 ft., but as D is 50 ft. above A, E is invisible from A.

By gradient :

$$\frac{50}{700 \times 3} = \frac{1}{42} \qquad\qquad \frac{75}{1520 \times 3} = \frac{1}{60}$$

Therefore E is invisible from A.

From all this certain rules can be deduced :—

1. If the map shows two points on opposite sides of a valley standing well above any intervening ground, they will be inter-visible.

2. If, between two points, a feature is represented higher than both, those two points will not be inter-visible.

3. If, between two points, a feature is represented higher than the lower of those two points, the points may or may not be inter-visible.

4. In a convex slope, two points on it will not be inter-visible.

5. When a slope is shown as concave, two points on it will probably be inter-visible.

6. When ground is shown to be level, inter-visibility will depend entirely upon trees, houses, etc.

Having digested so much, let us now delve further and confront any possible difficulties and complications.

Continental maps are usually contoured in metres.

$$1 \text{ metre} = 3 \text{ ft. } 3 \text{ in. } (39 \text{ in.}).$$

To convert metres to yards, add 10 per cent. ; to convert yards to metres, deduct 10 per cent.

Remember, 440 yds. = 400 metres.

On French maps V.Is. are usually—

5 metres = 16 ft. 4 in. = 16½ ft. = 5½ yds. roughly.

10 metres = 10 yds. 2½ ft. roughly.

In close contouring the position of your loophole is important.

Imagine your loophole is 5 ft. high—*i.e.*, 1·7 yds.

Take this example :—

$$AC = 360 \text{ yds.} ; \quad CB = 380 \text{ yds.}$$

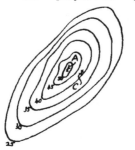

Take a point C between contours 40 and 45. See if B is visible from your loophole A.

Note.—V.I. of $BC = 30$ to $40 = 10$ metres.

Position of C estimated at 2 metres above 40 metre contour.

Therefore $10 + 2 = 12$ metres. Add 10 per cent. to convert to yards $= 13 \cdot 2$ yds.

V.I. of $AC = 50 - 42 = 8$ metres.

Add 10 per cent. to convert to yards $= 8 \cdot 8$ yds.

Add height of loophole, *i.e.*, $1 \cdot 7$ yds. $= 10 \cdot 5$ yds.

$$\text{Gradient of } CB \ \frac{1 \cdot 32}{380} = 1/28 \cdot 8.$$

$$\text{Gradient of } AC \ \frac{10 \cdot 5}{360} = 1/34 \cdot 3.$$

Gradient of CB is greater than gradient of AC, therefore A and B are not mutually visible.

BEARINGS, USE OF PROTRACTOR, RESECTION, WIDTH OF RIVER.

Bearings.

True North	...	Direction of North Pole from observer.
Grid North	...	Direction in which grid lines point towards top of map. Rectangular.
Magnetic North		Where magnetic needle points; *i.e.*, direction of magnetic pole from any point. Changes annually.

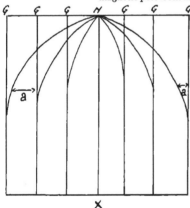

NX = Standard Meridian.

N = North Pole.

G = Grid North.

a = Angle of Convergency.

Note.—Standard Meridian = Greenwich.

67

Conversion of Bearings : Diagram and Rules.

1. GRID EAST OF TRUE.

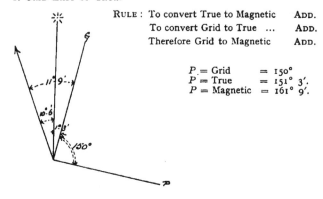

RULE : To convert True to Magnetic   ADD.
        To convert Grid to True   ...   ADD.
        Therefore Grid to Magnetic   ADD.

P = Grid   = 150°
P = True   = 151° 3′.
P = Magnetic   = 161° 9′.

2. GRID WEST OF TRUE.

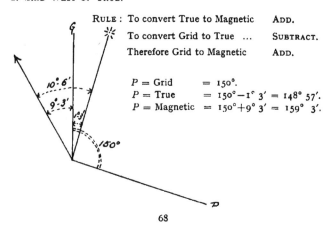

RULE : To convert True to Magnetic   ADD.
        To convert Grid to True   ...   SUBTRACT.
        Therefore Grid to Magnetic   ADD.

P = Grid   = 150°.
P = True   = 150° − 1° 3′ = 148° 57′.
P = Magnetic   = 150° + 9° 3′ = 159° 3′.

68

Required : 1/25,000 Maps and Protractors.

DIAGRAM AND RULE.

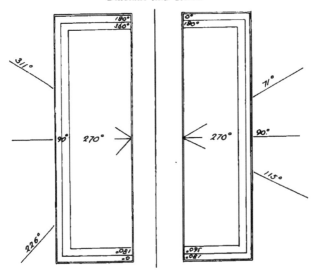

Bearings from 180° to 360°
marked on **inside.**

Bearings from 0° to 180°
marked on **outside.**

Back Bearings marked on **outside.**

Back bearings marked on **inside.**

Revision.

Setting Map.

1. Compass.

Magnetic needle coincident with Magnetic North line.

2. By Objects.

(a) Own position identified on map. Identify distant object on ground also known on map. Join two points on map and set by eye.

BEARING BY WATCH.—Point hour hand at sun ; half-way between hour hand and 12 o'clock is DUE SOUTH.

(b) Railways, roads, canals, etc. Two points in line on ground, map set to coincide.

Resection.

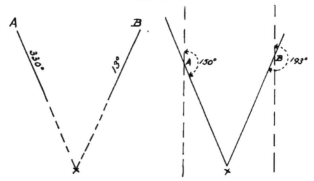

To find exact position of *x* on the ground. With compass take forward bearings on two known objects on map and ground *A* and *B*. Then, with protractor plot back bearings on the map from *A* and *B*.

$$x = \text{point of intersection.}$$

RULE.

If forward bearing less than 180°, add 180° to find back bearing.

If forward bearing more than 180°, subtract 180° to find back bearing.

In plotting back bearings, mark in magnetic meridians at *A* and *B*. At *A* put protractor on map right way up with arrow pointing $<$ and read outside figure. At *B* put it with arrow pointing $>$ and read inside figure.

Crossing the River.

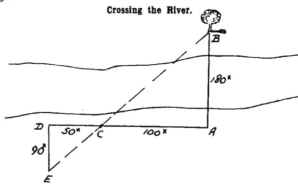

A = own position. Mark it. Select *B*, an object on opposite bank. Move off at right-angles and pace, say, 100 yds. Mark point *C*. Go on half as far again, 50 yds. Then turn at right-angles again and walk away from the river until you bring the marks at C and B into line. Count the paces while doing so. Distance paced since turning (D to E) will be one-half the width of the river.

SCALES AND MAP ENLARGEMENT.

Scales.

The word '' Scale '' means the relation which the length between any two points on a map bears to the horizontal distance between the same two points on the ground—*i.e.*, if the distance between two farmhouses on the map is 1 in. and the horizontal distance over the ground is two miles, the scale of the map is 1 in. to two miles.

'' Scale '' also equals a line drawn on the map suitably divided so that measurements of distance can be made from it on the map in question.

Expression of Scale.

1. In words—*i.e.*, '' so many inches to the mile,'' *or* '' so many miles to the inch.''

'' Miles to the inch '' for smaller scales than 1 in.; '' Inches to the mile '' for scales larger than 1 in.—*i.e.*, the relation between any unit on the map and any other unit on the ground.

2. By the representative fraction—*i.e.*, the R.F. which expresses the same thing in terms of a fraction with 1 as the numerator, the denominator being expressed in the same unit—*e.g.*, 1/20,000. The relation expressed by the fraction remains unaltered whatever the unit may be.

EXAMPLE.—By using the R.F. the relation in scale between two different maps can be established at once.

    (1) Scale 1/63,360 (*i.e.*, 1 in. to the mile); 1 in. represents 63,360 inches (*i.e.*, one mile).

    (2) Scale 1/100,000 (*i.e.*, 1 centimetre represents 100,000 cms.= 1 kilometre); 1 in. represents 100,000 in.=1·58 miles.

If only the R.F. is given, the number of inches to the mile or miles to the inch can be found as follows :—

To find the number of **miles** on the ground corresponding **to one inch** on the map, divide the denomination of the R.F. by 63,360.

    e.g., $1/100,000 = \dfrac{100,000}{63,360} = 1·58$ miles to the inch.

To find the number of inches on the map corresponding to one mile on the ground, divide 63,360 by the denominator of the R.F.—

    e.g., $1/100,000 = \dfrac{63,360}{100,000} = ·63$ in. to the mile.

It is useful to remember as a guide that 1/1,000,000 (called 1/M) is equivalent to 15·78 miles (approximately 16) to the inch. Hence 1/250,000 is about 4 miles to the inch.

NOTE.—Thus a 1/20,000 map is **four** times the size in scale of a 1/40,000 map, not twice the size.

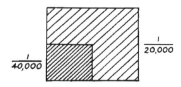

The scale on a map can usually be found by looking at the bottom of the map. This is usually given in three ways—

    (1) By the written word—*e.g.*, one inch to one statute mile.

    (2) By the R.F.—*e.g.*, 1/63,360.

    (3) By the drawn scale (primaries and secondaries).

NOTE.—In order to find the number of inches to the mile from the example given earlier :—

divide 63,360 by 25,000

i.e., $\dfrac{63,360}{25,000}$, which is 2·534 inches to the mile.

You may think that all this is unnecessarily complex, which of course it is. The reason for this is because in England we work in terms of inches, feet, yards and miles, whilst on the Continent they work in units of tens—*i.e.*, centimetres, metres and kilometres.

This brings you down to the question of what size map you are going to draw if you find yourself in the position of having to draw your own map to scale.

The problem of the choice of scale then comes in.

Here are some points to be remembered about military maps in general :—

    (1) The standard scale for operations is 1 in. to the mile.

    (2) Large-scale maps (2½ to 3 in. to the mile) are issued for pre-arranged operation in war. Note 1/20,000 is 3·17 in. to the mile.

    (3) Small-scale maps, (¼ in. to the mile) are issued for special mobile operations.

Now for a field sketch, or a sketch of an existing trench system— the sort of sketch you may find yourself having to do. The best scale to use will vary from 1 to 6 in. to the mile, or even more.

Always remember, however, that a scale of 2 in. to the mile will take up **four times** and not two times the amount of paper that a scale of 1 in. to the mile will take.

More detail can be given the larger the scale, less detail the smaller ; and therefore the larger the scale, the more accurate must be the detail.

Map Enlargement.

General idea of enlarging by eye is to copy the detail shown in a small figure (square, triangle) on the map into a similar but larger figure on fresh paper. Usually done by squares because the map is already squared. Draw in diagonals : the Union Jack method. If diagonals drawn in, other lines may be added by joining up the points at which diagonals intersect each other. By drawing all these lines the map will be divided into small triangles.

Keep to the grid squares and their diagonals—the easiest way ; remember the paper must be divided up in the same way and detail sketched in by eye.

EXAMPLE.—To enlarge a map to 4 in. to 1 mile. The large grid squares are 10,000 yds., each small square 1,000 yds. The ratio is 1 : 4 ; thus sides of grid on enlargement must be 40,000 yds., as measured on the 1-in. grid. Prick through from the 1-in. map on to the paper on which enlargement is to be made the corners of a 40,000-yds. (1 in.) grid and draw lines through holes. Add diagonals to both original and enlargement and copy details by eye.

Scale 1 in. to 1 mile.   Scale 4 in. to 1 mile.

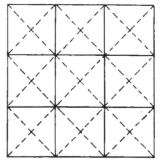

NOTE.—The enlargement is 16 times bigger (4 × 4) than the original.

USE OF COMPASS

Required : Compasses and piece of cardboard.

Liquid Prismatic Compass.

The advantage of this type is that the card, being immersed in liquid, settles much quicker than the Mark VIII. Much the same as Mark VIII, but outer graduation on card transparent. A luminous patch on bottom of box beneath erected prism illuminates graduation at night. On the glass which seals the liquid is another luminous patch near hinge ; on this horizontal patch the lubber line is drawn. Setting circle etched on upper glass and with milled edge. The bearing is then set for night marching by bringing the desired reading on the upper glass into coincidence with the lubber line.

Note that in the graduation (5°) the short division traces correspond to the figures. There is, however, a setting vane for use with the points of the compass, the only external graduation ; corresponding to this setting vane, there is a luminous direction mark on the movable upper glass. Bubbles in the liquid may be trapped by turning compass over and slowly turning it back again.

If a star chosen, for choice Polaris as others always changing position. An error of 5°=150 yards per mile of march.

To march on Compass after Setting.

Keep luminous direction mark on movable upper glass coincident with the luminous diamond on the compass card and march on the lubber line. You will then be marching on the set bearing. To take a bearing read the outside figure on the compass card.

Use of Compass.

Setting and reading bearings. (See footnote to this page.)
Disturbance : Steel helmet, 3 yards. Respirator must be in slung position.

To test Compass.

Take bearings on map of two points ; say, take bearing of B from A. If compass accurate, difference should be 180° between forward and back bearings of the above.

    (1) Identify on map and ground point A and some distant object B.
    (2) From map with protractor find True or Grid bearing of B from A.
    (3) With compass read bearing of B.
    (4) Difference between Grid and Compass bearings should equal Magnetic Variation.

NOTE.—As it is possible to obtain so many books of instruction, manuals, etc., which give detailed instruction in the use of the compass, the author considered it desirable to curtail the above notes.

Negotiating an Obstacle.

METHOD 1.—Send someone round to the other side of the obstacle, halt him when on the bearing. Walk round to him and continue on march. The distance must be taken into account.

METHOD 2.—*Right-angled* and *left-angled* bearings—*i.e.*, negotiating an obstacle.

Rule : To the *Right*, ADD.

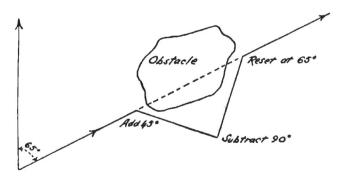

Rule : To the *Left*, SUBTRACT.

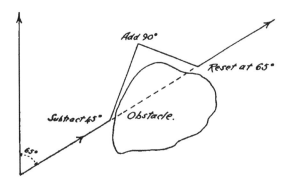

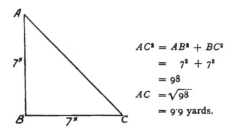

$$AC^2 = AB^2 + BC^2$$
$$= 7^2 + 7^2$$
$$= 98$$
$$AC = \sqrt{98}$$
$$= 9\cdot9 \text{ yards.}$$

Compass March by Night (Treasure Hunt).

To Lay Out.

Take a piece of graph paper. Put a drawing pin at the starting and finishing points.

NOTE.—The key bearing between them must be taken previously, paced and secretly marked.

Have a piece of loose string with ends fixed at starting and finishing points. Then with two more pins move the string about. You will thus get three different bearings, all of approximately the same distance and they can be measured with the protractor.

Procedure.

Hand courses to leaders. Men will act as patrols, particularly when courses cross and/or they see each other.

JUDGING DISTANCE

Judging distance is extremely important to the sniper, whose marksmanship might be nullified by an error in judging distance ; also to the scout or observer, whose information must be accurate to be useful.

The sniper has to hit with one shot, and must be trained to judge accurately up to 600 yds. at least ; the scout and observer to even longer distances, and lateral distances also.

Methods :—

        (1) Judging distance.
        (2) Range-finders
        (3) Large-scale maps   }   often not available.

NOTE.—Check by observation of fire when possible.

Methods of Judging Distance.
        (1) Unit of measure.
        (2) Appearance.

1. Unit 100 yds.—Mental yard measure. Can be used only up to 300 yds. (or 400 yds. under favourable conditions) when all the ground between observer and object can be seen.

2. Appearance.—What objects look like and amount of detail visible at different distances. Objects of known size such as men or an ordinary house door are best, but objects of unknown size are useful if a study of the detail visible is made.

A general guide only can be given owing to differences in eyesight, so everyone must make his own scale of visibility. In both methods varying conditions of light, background and country must be taken into account, and practice be given therein.

Objects look farther away when difficult to see and nearer when easy to see.

In training do not allow guessing and ask for reasons for and methods used in estimates.

Gradually shorten the time allowed for judging.

Aids to Judging Distance.
Halving.—Judging to a point half-way and doubling. Dangerous, because an error in the first estimate will be doubled in the full estimate.

77

Bracketing.—Estimating the longest and shortest range possible and taking the mean.

Averaging.—When sniper and observer or other pairs or more are working together, both or all estimate and take the mean.

Key Range.—When the range to an object is known, other objects approximately in the same arc may be judged by comparison with the key range.

Range Cards.—An article of store carried in the field. In defence all ranges obtained should be recorded thereon, and every sniper's post should have one.

How to Use.

1. At bottom accurately describe your position, method of obtaining ranges, your name and date. A weather note might be useful.

2. Put in the range to be represented by each semi-circle.

3. Choose an unmistakable object in the sector and draw a thick settle ray to it.

4. Keeping the card on the setting ray, draw rays in the direction of the selected objects to the distance on the card.

5. Write in BLOCK LETTERS horizontally a short description of each object as seen by the naked eye, and its range at the end of its ray.

To use card, raise it to eye-level and direct the setting ray on the object named ; once set, all objects ranged can be identified by an observer.

Remember, neatness, block letters, and horizontal descriptions and distances.

MUSKETRY AND TELESCOPIC SIGHTS

MUSKETRY.

Practical Hints for Snipers.

Causes of Inaccuracy in Shooting.

 (1) Faults in the Rifle.
 (2) Faults in the Sights.
 (3) Faults in the Ammunition.
 (4) Personal Error.

1. FAULTS IN THE RIFLE.

 (a) Worn-out barrel (usually from neglect in cleaning).
 (b) Worn-out bolt.
 (c) Warped or bent fore-end.
 (d) Metallic or nickel fouling.
 (e) Faulty trigger pull—too heavy or too light a pull.

2. FAULTS IN THE SIGHTS.

 (a) Damaged foresight, too thin, highly polished, etc.
 (b) Damaged backsight or not properly adjusted—slips.
 (c) Movement of windgauge, loose.

3. FAULTS IN THE AMMUNITION.

 (a) Select one brand and keep to it if possible.
 (b) Different ammunition gives different elevations—as much as three minutes per 100 yards.
 (c) Do not expose cartridges to sun or heat.
 (d) Keep ammunition clean and dry and free from oil.

Ammunition Markings.—E., Eley; K.N., King's Norton; K., Kynoch; R.L., Royal Laboratory; G., Greenwood & Batley; B., Birmingham Munitions Co.; W., Winchester; J., Joyce; N., Nobel; P., Peters; D.C., Dominion of Canada; U., Union Metallic Co.; U.S., U.S. Cartridge Co.

British Bullet.—British ordinary bullet held in position by three nicks or indentations.

American Bullet.—American bullet gripped all round.

German Bullet.—German bullet easily removed and reversed for penetrating purposes.

Tracer Ammunition.—Made by Royal Laboratory. No indentations on case and letter " G " on base of case.

4. PERSONAL ERROR.

   (a) *Aiming.*

       (i) To look generally along the sights so as to bring them approximately in line with each other and with the mark.

      (ii) To focus alternately the backsight and the foresight till satisfied that they are in their proper relative positions.

    (iii) To bring the foresight to the correct point on the mark while endeavouring to maintain it and the backsight in their correct positions.

    (iv) Rapidly to check the position of the foresight in relation to the backsight.

     (v) To check and correct the position of the foresight on the target and to fire the shot.

    (vi) The human eye is accountable for a general error in accuracy of sighting of 1 in. for every 100 yds. range.

These processes in reality only take a very short time, but are most important to observe if accurate shooting is desired.

COMMON FAULTS IN AIMING.

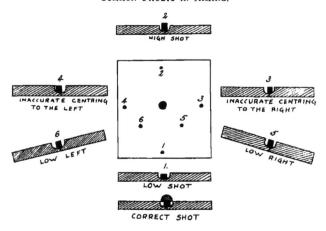

   (b) *Position must be comfortable.*

   (c) *Holding.*

       (i) Hold with both hands ; most important. Bad holding is most prevalent.

      (ii) It must be remembered that the same rifle in different hands will shoot quite differently. This is due to peculiarities in holding.

(iii) Sniping rifles will be used sometimes by one man, sometimes by another, and no man must be surprised if in the hands of one man the rifle shoots a little to the right whilst in the hands of another it shoots a little left, high or low, etc. Each man must learn for himself where the rifle shoots in his own hands.

(iv) It has been continually noticed at Bisley that two of the best-known shots may shoot with the same rifle, and one invariably put his shots 1 or 2 in. per 100 yds. to the left or right of the other. The difference will be constant.

(v) If a rifle is so held that the whole of the recoil is taken on the heel for one shot and the whole of the recoil on the toe for the next shot, a considerable difference will be found in the elevation ; and different men vary considerably in the way they take the recoil. Every man must try to take it in the same manner for every shot or he will not keep his elevation.

(d) *Trigger Pressing.*

(i) This should be constantly practised ; it is most important.

(ii) Take up the first pull directly you are on the target. Men are apt to take up both pulls at once, which is fatal to good shooting.

(iii) If the rifle is new, always press the trigger several times before going down on firing-point.

(e) *Resting Rifle.*—Always rest it at the same place and lightly. Resting a rifle **lightly** makes no practical difference to the shooting, but nine men out of ten do not rest it lightly ; they do not support the weight of rifle with left hand, but, on the contrary, drag it down heavily on to the rest. With a rifle so held down the bullet will strike 3½ in. per 100 yds. higher if the rest be taken at the nosecap, and half this amount if the rest be taken at the band. This fact applies particularly to snipers firing through loopholes in steel plates and resting nosecap.

Rifle Cleaning.

1. Fouling : For fouling use rags and oil or boiling water.
2. Rust : For rust use oil and gauze, motty paste.
3. Nickelling : Use K.N. Solvent, motty paste.
4. Rub oil well into woodwork to prevent warping.
5. Test all screws.

Shooting Hints.

1. Oily or wet barrel : Bullet generally goes high, causes smoke.
2. In heavy rain bullet generally goes high.
3. With hot barrel bullet goes low.
4. Wrong bolt : Erratic shooting.
5. Morning and evening shoot may differ several minutes in elevation.

6. When unloading do not force bolt back and forward too strenuously. It tends to loosen and wear bolt head and spoil pull-off.

7. When a shot is fired, immediately open bolt, let gas out and leave bolt open until all is ready for next shot. This prevents foul gases " stewing " in the barrel, allows barrel to cool and obviates cartridges being fired at various temperatures.

8. Change of light—
    (a) Open sights : Lights up, sights up ; lights down, sights down.
    (b) Does not affect telescopic sights.

9. In case of obstruction in barrel, such as a broken pull-through, hold the rifle butt upwards and fill barrel full with water and fire a blank cartridge.

10. The life of a barrel depends more on cleaning than on use, and every man keen on shooting knows this. Take an expert rifle shot or an old hunter and watch his methods ; his rifle is a living thing to him, particularly the bore.

11. When polishing do not use wire gauze on a new barrel. If necessary polish may be partially renewed by using Brooke's soap. Damp a flannelette patch and rub a little on it.

12. Bulges are caused by allowing an obstruction to get into the barrel, such as earth, snow, putting in wooden or cloth plug, etc.

13. Never polish the sights on a rifle.

14. Avoid oil in breach and on bolt head. Remove all oil from bore before firing. Snipers must be particular to remember this as oil greatly increases flash and thereby gas.

15. No matter how free the rifle may be from oil, there is always a tendency for the first few shots with Mk. VII ammunition through a clean barrel to go a little higher than the subsequent shots. At 200 yards the second may be an inch lower than the first, the third down another inch, the fourth down the same amount ; then the elevation holds constant.

Final Hints.

1. Test the rifle as often as possible.

2. The Sniper must know his rifle and its peculiarities.

3. It is impossible to over-estimate the great value of snapping practice.

4. If given an opportunity always procure suitable-length stock.

5. Always use your own bolt.

Elevation.

1. When firing up or down hill use less elevation.

2. If firing vertically up or down use sights at 200 yards.

3. When snipers visit a range to test rifles for elevation the result should be carefully marked down in a note-book in case the rifle has to be transferred to another sniper.

ELEVATION TABLES.

(a) *Going Up.*—For a low shot multiply the distance you are at by the next higher. This scale is approximately correct and can easily be remembered.

	Going Up : Low Shot.	Going Down : High Shot.
yds.	in.	in.
100 to 200 ...	— 3½	4
200 to 300 ...	— 7	9
300 to 400 ...	— 12	16
400 to 500 ...	— 20	25
500 to 600 ...	— 28	36
600 to 700 ...	— 40	49
700 to 800 ...	— 54	64
800 to 900 ...	— 72	81
900 to 1,000 ...	— 94	100

(b) *Going Down.*—When going down multiply the range you are at by itself to obtain correct elevation. Example : to 100 yds. from 800 yds, the difference is, as can be seen by the table, 64 in.

(c) The following is another formula very similar to the above table which is also easy to remember and approximately correct :—

To hit the target higher at the same range by raising sight 100 yds., multiply the first figure of the range you are at by the first figure of the next range ; result, in inches, is point bullet will strike. If at 200 yds. and sights raised to 300 yds., $2 \times 3 = 6$ in. higher.

If the sights are moved more than 100 yds, add the first figure of the higher ranges together and multiply by the first figure of range you are shooting at. If at 200 yds. and sights raised to 500 yds, $3 + 4 + 5 = 12 \times 2 = 24$ in.

To hit the target lower at the same range by lowering sight 100 yds., multiply first figure of range you are at by itself. If at 300 yds. and you lower sights to 200 yds., $3 \times 3 = 9$ in. lower.

If the sight is moved more than 100 yds., add the first figure of the lower range, less the lowest, to the first figure of the lower range you are shooting at, and multiply by it. If at 500 yds. and sights are lowered to 200 yds., $3 + 4 + 5 = 12 \times 5 = 60$ in. lower.

Angle of Tilt.

Sights must be kept perfectly upright. If tilted the bullet goes low and towards the side to which the sights are inclined.

Angle of Tilt.	Range.	Bullet Strikes	
		Sideways.	Low.
15°	300	8 in.	1 in.
	600	3 ft. 5 in.	5 in.
	900	9 ft. 3 in.	1 ft. 4 in.

Rise of Bullet.

Maximum rise of bullet at a distance a little beyond half-way :—

```
Firing at 200 yds.  ...   Rises        5 in.  ⎫
   ,,     500  ,,    ...    ,,   3 ft. 10 in.  ⎪  above
   ,,     600  ,,    ...    ,,   6 ft.  5 in.  ⎬  the
   ,,     800  ,,    ...    ,,  13 ft.  6 in.  ⎪  line of
   ,,     900  ,,    ...    ,,  19 ft. 10 in.  ⎭  sights.
   ,,    1000  ,,    ...    ,,  25 ft.
```

Initial spin of the bullet is at the rate of 2,640 revolutions per second or 144,000 revolutions per minute.

Jump.

Rifles have a vertical as well as a horizontal jump, which may vary more or less with each competitor, thus giving rise to different elevations being required for this cause alone if two competitors use the same rifle.

The horizontal side jump to the left when the shot is from the right shoulder is allowed for (in the case of all Government rifles) by placing the foresight out of centre, the barleycorn being .023 in. from the centre of the block, to the left.

JUMP WHEN FIRED FROM A FIXED REST.

```
                     ft. in.
     200 yds.   ...   1   8   ⎫
     500  ,,    ...   4   2   ⎪
     600  ,,    ...   5   0   ⎬  on target.
     800  ,,    ...   6   8   ⎪
     900  ,,    ...   7   6   ⎭
   1,000  ,,    ...   8   4
```

The jump is considerably less when fired from the shoulder, and is usually constant with each competitor.

Deflection.

. The deflection of the bullet due to the twist of the rifling in the barrel is approximately 1 ft. to the left at 1,000 yds.

Aiming Off for Movement.

Three rules—

(1) Get an accurate aim on the mark.

(2) Carry the aim forward to the estimated distance in front of the mark and maintain the aim on this point by swinging the rifle.

(3) Press the trigger so as to discharge the rifle without checking the swing.

Rule (1) is necessary because loss of elevation may occur if the aim is not first taken on the mark.

Rule (2) marks the second step. The aim is just to swing forward and then keep moving to correspond with the movement of the target.

Rule (3). The need for this is paramount and it holds the secret of successful shooting at moving objects, as will be explained.

The allowance necessary for a mark moving at a given speed, at a given distance, is quite simple to calculate. It depends on two things :—

(1) The time taken by the bullet to traverse the distance from the muzzle to the mark, and

(2) The amount by which the mark will in that time have shifted its position.

Velocity : Mk. VII, 2,440 ft. per second.

ALLOWANCE FOR TIME OF FLIGHT.

The times of flight of Mk. VII bullet up to 600 yds. are as follows :—

100 yds.	...	0.13 seconds (13 hundredths).
200 ,,	...	0.26 ,,
300 ,,	...	0.42 ,,
400 ,,	...	0.59 ,,
500 ,,	...	0.79 ,,
600 ,,	...	1.00 ,,

It is quite simple to calculate the movement. Add one-half to the speed of the mark in miles per hour and you get the number of feet it moves in a second. Thus :—

4 m.p.h. is	6 ft. per second	(a fast walk).
8 m.p.h. is	12 ,, ,,	(a run).
12 m.p.h. is	18 ,, ,,	(a fast run ; normal speed of tank),
15 m.p.h. is	22 ,, ,,	(speed of light tank).

We can now calculate the amount of movement at these speeds during the time the bullet takes to traverse the various distances.

Range.	4 m.p.h.	8 m.p.h.	12 m.p.h.	15 m.p.h.
100	9 in.	1 ft. 5 in.	2 ft. 2 in.	2 ft. 6 in.
200	1 ft. 6 in.	3 ft. 1 in.	4 ft. 7 in.	5 ft. 8 in.
300	2 ft. 5 in.	4 ft. 10 in.	7 ft. 3 in.	9 ft. 3 in.
400	3 ft. 5 in.	6 ft. 11 in.	10 ft. 4 in.	14 ft. 0 in.
500	4 ft. 8 in.	9 ft. 4 in.	13 ft. 4 in.	17 ft. 0 in.
600	5 ft. 10 in.	11 ft. 8 in.	17 ft. 6 in.	22 ft. 0 in.

It should be noted that the sequence for 8 m.p.h. runs nearly 1½, 3, 5, 7, 9, 12 ft. It is considered to be almost useless to fire a single shot at an individual man in motion beyond about 300 yds.

The allowances given above depend on the rifle pointing to the right place when the bullet actually leaves the muzzle.

There is, however, a natural tendency to check the swing of the rifle as the trigger is released or as the decision to press the trigger is finally communicated from brain to forefinger. Now if this is done a small but important interval of time is brought into play before the bullet leaves the rifle. Several things occur which will take time, even if only a very short time. These are :—

(1) The final pressure of the finger on the trigger.

(2) The travel forward of the cocking-piece after the sear is released.

(3) The ignition of the cap.

(4) The travel of the bullet to the muzzle.

If it be assumed that the processes take altogether one-tenth of a second, additional allowances will be required as under :—

At 4 m.p.h. ... 0.6 ft. irrespective of distance.

At 8 m.p.h. ... 1.2 ft. ,, ,, ,,

At 12 m.p.h. ... 1.8 ft. ,, ,, ,,

At 15 m.p.h. ... 2.3 ft. ,, ,, ,,

Therefore if the rifle is checked when the trigger is released a larger allowance is needed. This is most easily done if the shot is fired standing and the whole of the upper part of the body swung round on the hips. The arms should not be swung, but should partake of the movement of the body. **This position is not often practicable.**

The sitting position is also good for getting a swing.

The lying position is difficult ; firing at a moving object with the elbows on the ground requires some practice.

A swing cannot be used if the mark is only seen crossing a narrow opening in the parapet of a trench, etc. In such cases it is rather a matter of snap-shooting at a point in front of the crossing target.

DIAGONAL MOVEMENT.

We have dealt so far only with movement across the line of fire, but this is not the only case. Diagonal movement—*i.e.*, when the mark is approaching or receding as well as crossing—may be frequent. The principle in such cases is quite simple, and the aim must be directed the necessary number of feet in front, just as in a crossing shot, but remembering that the allowance must be made in the direction in which the mark is moving so that the bullet and the mark may meet.

When the target is getting farther away or coming nearer, the elevation must, of course, be reasonably correct on the range at which the shot is fired.

Under-estimate rather than over-estimate a range. The strike of the bullet will be seen and facilitate correction, also chance of ricochet.

The Bullet.

A bullet travels 600 yds. in first second,
           400 yds. in second second,
           300 yds. in third second.

A bullet revolves at 2,640 revolutions per second at muzzle.

Greatest height attained by bullet, 9,200 ft., taking 17 seconds to go up and 45 seconds to come down, still spinning and base first.

Greatest range, 3,400 yds. (Mk. VII ammunition).

Pressure of explosion, 10 tons to square inch.

Bayonet fixed, Mk. VII ammunition hits high, from 1 ft. 6 in. at 200 yds. to 4 ft. at 600 yds.

Never accept another man's sighting ; test the rifle yourself.

TELESCOPIC SIGHTS.

The use of telescopic sights is not new in warfare ; they were used in the Indian Mutiny, 1856 ; the American Civil War, 1865 ; and at Bisley, 1900.

Telescopic sights do not increase accuracy very much. They will not make a marksman out of a bad shot, but merely enable aim to be taken at small and indistinct objects.

Aiming.—Always aim at six o'clock line of object ; be careful to aim correctly. More care is required in aiming with telescopic sights than with open sights.

Holding.—The telescopic sight is often mounted on the side of the rifle, and the head therefore loses steadying support of butt. To remedy, tie a pad or screw a piece of wood on left side of butt.

Snapping Practice.—Snapping practice, and lots of it, is very necessary in order to accustom men to their rifles and improving hold and let-off.

Telescopic Sights—

    (*a*) Must never be taken to pieces.

    (*b*) Have from eight to twelve lenses.

    (*c*) The front lens is called the object glass.

    (*d*) Rear lens is eye-piece.

    (*e*) The pointer and cross hair are called the reticule.

In aiming the eye should be 4 in. to $4\frac{1}{2}$ in. from eye-piece.

NOTE.—Each telescopic sight is fitted to a particular rifle and must be used with that rifle and with no other on any account.

Simple Rules for Use and Care of T.S.

Focus.

The telescope should be carefully focused. This is done by loosening the capstan head on the sleeve on top of the barrel of the telescope and moving the sleeve to right or left as necessary. This method varies with some telescopic sights.

When the focus has been found, screw up the capstan head or screw holding the sleeve.

Elevation.

The elevation is altered by using the elevation drum on top of the telescope. When the elevation drum has been moved to the desired position it should be fixed in that position by tightening the screw.

Aim.

The aim is taken by sighting the object aimed at on the top of the pointer in the telescope—*i.e.*, aiming at six o'clock.

Screws and Lenses.

Men using telescopic sights should be strictly forbidden to touch any screws, capstan heads, etc., at all except the capstan head on the focusing sleeve and range dial screw. **They must make no attempt to clean the lenses,** and must only carefully polish the outside of the eye-piece and object glass, neither of which must be unscrewed.

The polishing should be done with a clean handkerchief and must on no account scratch the glass.

Lenses should never be taken out to clean, otherwise the shooting of the telescopic-sight rifle will be entirely altered.

Lateral Adjustment.

When absolutely necessary lateral adjustment can be obtained in the case of certain makes of telescopic sights (The Periscopic Company and some others) by tightening and loosening the capstan heads which are placed on either side of the barrel of the telescope just below the elevating drum.

If the rifle shoots to the right, first loosen left capstan head and then tighten right, and if it shoots to the left reverse the process. But this tightening and loosening should be most carefully done as it is a delicate operation.

Very roughly speaking, one half-turn equals 6 in. on the target at 100 yards, but this varies.

Fitting.

The front leg of the fitting by which the telescopic sight is fixed to the rifle is in some makes (Aldis Co's. telescopic sight, fitted by Purdey and others) made to fit into a dovetailed slot.

In order to correct the lateral shooting of these rifles, take out the screw on top which holds the dovetailed slot in place, and tap the dovetailed slot over until the rifle shoots correctly.

If the rifle shoots to the right, tap to the right to correct, and if to the left, tap more to the left to correct.

On a 4 in. base tapping $\frac{1}{100}$ in. equals 9 in. on the target at 100 yards.

A man who has proved himself capable of handling a telescopic-sight rifle should be allowed to use that rifle exclusively.

Telescopic sights should remain in a battalion and should never be handed over as trench stores.

The elevation and lateral zero of telescopic sights vary considerably in different men's hands. It is therefore necessary for a man to know the rifle with which he is shooting in order to be certain of any results.

Damp or Fogged Sights.

The telescopic sights in the hands of many of our snipers are not properly focused to the sight of the individual using them, and in other cases the object glass and lenses are fogged by damp through lack of care.

If a telescopic sight which is fogged with damp is kept in a warm room or exposed to the sun, the damp will evaporate, but telescopic sights should not be toasted at the fire recklessly or they will be ruined.

Few Shots.

As few shots as possible should be fired through telescopic rifles. After 300 to 500 shots have been fired, the extreme accuracy of the rifle begins to deteriorate.

THE P.14 RIFLE AND P.18 TELESCOPIC SIGHT

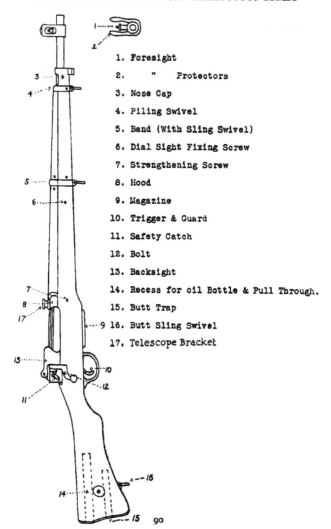

1. Foresight
2. " Protectors
3. Nose Cap
4. Piling Swivel
5. Band (With Sling Swivel)
6. Dial Sight Fixing Screw
7. Strengthening Screw
8. Hood
9. Magazine
10. Trigger & Guard
11. Safety Catch
12. Bolt
13. Backsight
14. Recess for oil Bottle & Pull Through.
15. Butt Trap
16. Butt Sling Swivel
17. Telescope Bracket

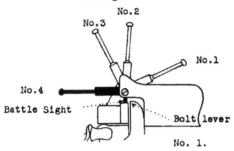

Diagram showing 4 Positions of
Backsight.

No.2

No.3

No.1

No.4

Battle Sight

Bolt lever

No. 1.

MAUSER ACTION P. 1914

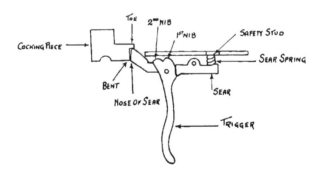

TOE 2ᴺᴰ NIB 1ˢᵀ NIB SAFETY STUD

COCKING PIECE

SEAR SPRING

BENT

NOSE OF SEAR

SEAR

TRIGGER

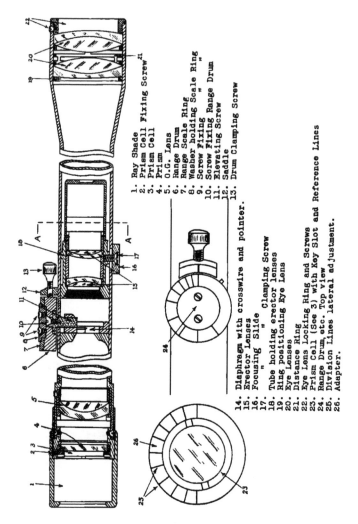

1. Ray Shade
2. Prism Cell Fixing Screw[21]
3. Prism Cell
4. Prism
5. O.G. Lens
6. Range Drum
7. Range Scale Ring
8. Washer holding Scale Ring
9. Screw Fixing   "
10. Screw Fixing Range Drum
11. Elevating Screw
12. Saddle
13. Drum Clamping Screw

14. Diaphragm with crosswire and pointer.
15. Erector Lenses
16. Focusing Slide
17.   "   "   Clamping Screw
18. Tube holding erector lenses
19. Ring positioning Eye Lens
20. Eye Lenses
21. Distance Ring
22. Eye Lens Locking Ring and Screws
23. Prism Cell (See 3) with Key Slot and Reference Lines
24. Range Drum, etc. Top view
25. Division Lines lateral adjustment.
26. Adapter.

Section on A. A.

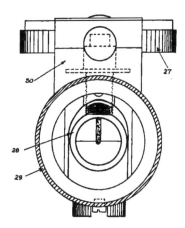

27. Range Drum (See 6 (1))

28. Cross Wire and Pointer in
    Diaphragm.

29. Telescope Tube

30. Saddle.

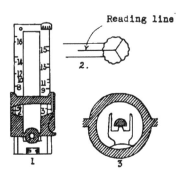

No. 2

Sights:
Enfield 1914 Rifle.

SNIPERS' POSTS, LOOPHOLES, OBSERVATION POSTS AND HIDES

Position.

Decide first of all what you want it for—

- (a) Observation, sniping, or for both purposes.
- (b) Whether it is to command a considerable field of view or some special point.
- (c) Do not trust to luck, but use the utmost care in the selection of the position.
- (d) If it is decided to use a sniping plate, precaution must be taken to set the plate at the right angle so that the loophole will cover the desired target. A couple of inches high or low makes all the difference ; it may cause the rifle to be pointed in the air or pointed to the ground in front of the parapet.

Points to be considered.

As many loopholes as possible should be constructed.

If dummy loopholes are made they should be placed at some distance from an occupied loophole, because if they are spotted the enemy may try to put the position out of action with a trench-mortar bombardment.

An even or well-built parapet is difficult for concealment of loopholes. There are several types which can be used, but great care must be taken in construction, particularly if front-line trenches are close together ; as a rule it will not be long before a parapet becomes damaged by shell fire.

An uneven or broken parapet provides many excellent opportunities for the construction of loopholes and observation posts ; it creates many shadows, and by reason of its rough appearance almost any type of loophole may be built. The Germans nearly always constructed uneven parapets, and in addition to this they scattered all kinds and descriptions of rubbish on the parapet, such as old clothes, boards, tin cans, barbed wire, shovels, picks, coloured sandbags, etc. ; the last named were particularly good for the concealment of observation posts and sniping posts. If coloured bags are used they must be distributed unevenly throughout a considerable length of parapet and not confined to one isolated spot, or the enemy would be certain to shoot it up.

Dummy loopholes and observation posts can be made of old cans, boots, black or white paint, fake holes, rat holes, etc. etc.

Front-Line Parapet.

ADVANTAGES.

Advantages in construction of observation posts and loopholes.

(a) Nearest to enemy lines.
(b) Sometimes the only available place.

DISADVANTAGES.

(a) Most carefully searched by the enemy.
(b) Therefore requires more careful concealment.
(c) Sometimes difficult to build owing to thickness or rotten condition of parapet.

Parados.

ADVANTAGES.

(a) Less easily detected.
(b) Not so easily searched as the front line.
(c) The gas from the discharge of the rifle is difficult to detect owing to smoke of braziers and a certain kind of mist or damp which always appears to exist between parados and parapet.

DISADVANTAGES.

(a) The parados in the first place must, of course, be built slightly higher than the parapet.
(b) The Germans had an unpleasant habit of continually stripping a high parados with shell fire, but the sniper can construct a few reserve loopholes there, which are very useful to fire from occasionally.

Traverse.

A certain number of sniping posts should always be constructed in traverses in both front and support lines in case of accidents ; namely, if the enemy made a raid into our front line at night, or early morning, a couple of snipers holding a commanding position in a traverse, with loopholes on either side, should be able to give a good account of themselves for a short time in any event, and might break up the raid altogether. Raids on a small scale must be carried out quickly to be successful. It was rarely a wise proceeding to remain more than a few minutes in the enemy trenches, so that a strong opposition from a certain number of well-placed and well-protected snipers or riflemen would have been invaluable on many occasions during the war.

Support, Communication and Reserve Trenches.

ADVANTAGES.

(a) Least watched or searched by the enemy.
(b) Usually easy of approach.
(c) A sap from a communication trench very often provides an excellent position for a sniping or observation post.

DISADVANTAGE.

Usually long distance from the enemy.

Reserve Trenches.—A certain number of loopholes should be built in all reserve trenches.

In Front of Parapet.

Sniping posts, etc., can be used in front of the parapet when—

(a) Trenches are far apart.

(b) The ground between trenches is not severely dominated by observation.

(c) The ground is at all favourable for sniping.

ADVANTAGES.

(a) Difficult for the enemy to locate if fire is masked from the parapet.

(b) Most difficult to spot a sniper or observer if " dug in."

(c) The enemy's parapet can be thoroughly searched for loopholes.

(d) Usually not difficult to conceal owing to the broken nature of the ground, shell holes, etc.

(e) It often gives a clear skyline shot.

(f) It is an easy matter to run out a sap from any disused trenches or excavations in front of the parapet.

(g) It can be used very effectively from positions in your own wire, in grass, etc., and is most difficult to spot.

DISADVANTAGE.

Cannot get out by day or get back unless there is a sap.

Points in Rear of the Front Line.

These afford the best sniping posts. The ground should be well reconnoitred to find the most suitable places, and if carefully concealed these will be most difficult for an enemy to locate.

Approach and Movement.

Always obtain daylight approach if possible.

(a) It enables a post to be occupied or left at any moment.

(b) Frequent reliefs can be made.

(c) If detected the occupants can usually retire in safety.

If daylight approach is impossible—

(a) Make the post as comfortable as possible on account of the long period which must elapse before a relief can be made.

(b) Make it sufficiently large for an observer, if possible.

(c) A good rest for the rifle and telescope and an easy firing position applies to all posts and hides. A sitting position is the easiest to maintain at all times, but it is not always possible to arrange this.

Cover.

There are two important considerations under this heading when selecting a post—

(a) Cover from **fire.**

(b) Cover from **view.**

One must not be sacrificed for the other. Good concealment should be used in preference to protection.

Exclusiveness.

Posts should be used exclusively by snipers and observers. This should be a Battalion Order.

They should be put out of bounds to everyone except those entitled to use them, particularly sentries and visitors in the front line.

Loopholes during the last war were frequently betrayed through idle curiosity.

It is most difficult to maintain exclusiveness of loopholes in the front line.

Precautions.

Do not use new loopholes too soon after construction ; wait a day or two and let them weather down a little, then try a single shot and await result. The sniper will soon know whether he has been spotted or not.

Do not forget the danger of gas from your rifle giving your position away. It shows most in damp or misty days. This is also increased or decreased according to the ammunition used. The sniper must be particularly careful when firing from a position in the front line.

Always mask the face when under observation by the enemy.

Avoid all unnecessary movement in daylight ; even in the open, if a man keeps still he is difficult to spot.

Do not smoke or use fires or candles in observation posts or sniping posts. If restless chew gum or tobacco.

It is most important to remember to use curtains over the entrance to sniping and observation posts, and to use " gags," which usually consist of a sandbag rolled up and inserted in the opening in the observation post or loophole, every time the post is vacated.

The post must be entered and the curtain replaced before the " gag " is removed from the loophole ; if this is not done there will be great danger of light showing through and giving the location away to the enemy. A ground sheet or thick piece of canvas makes the best curtain ; sand-bagging is too thin—the light shows through.

If a post or loophole is discovered it should be abandoned or, better still, dismantled or filled up. It us hardly ever advisable to occupy a spotted position, notwithstanding the fact that different units frequently come in in front of your positions. The fact of a sniping post having been spotted is certain to be passed on in Intelligence Reports from one unit to another.

Never use a rifle with a highly polished barrel ; cover it with sacking, tape, brown paint, or mud, etc.

Never use ordinary service caps when under observation ; use masks, hoods, sacking, veils or woollen caps, something without a distinct outline.

Avoid wearing anything that glitters or shines.

Much precaution should be exercised when taking over a front line for the first time from another unit. A careful examination must be made of all posts and hides. It is always safe to assume that the last occupant of the post has been careless. Many things can happen.

Opportunities for Construction.

Loopholes can be made at night ; if the construction presents a certain amount of difficulty, the working party should be large enough to complete the post before daylight or else to camouflage the work in such a way that no trace of the night's work will be visible when daylight appears. Posts can sometimes be conveniently constructed when parapets have been breached by shell fire, or on misty or foggy days.

Construction of various types of posts should be practised behind the lines when the battalion is at rest ; mistakes can then be noted and rectified.

It is unlikely that an important post can be constructed successfully on a dark night unless it has been built first of all in daylight.

SNIPERS' POSTS, LOOPHOLES, OBSERVATION POSTS AND HIDES AND HOW TO BUILD THEM.

Loopholes.

No. 1 Loophole.

Used principally in what are called " R.E. parapets," being those built by Engineer working parties. The bags were all evenly laid, thereby increasing the difficulty in concealment of loopholes. It was also difficult to bring anything but direct fire to bear on the enemy's lines from any of these loopholes. The dummy bags sewn on the plate restricted the view and field of fire.

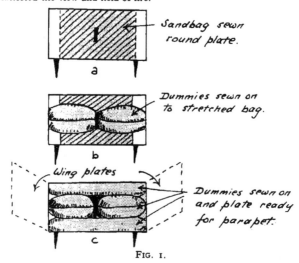

Sandbag sewn round plate.

Dummies sewn on to stretched bag.

Wing plates

Dummies sewn on and plate ready for parapet.

FIG. 1.

In Fig. 1c dotted lines represent what are called " wing " plates, which are ordinary sniping plates placed at an angle from the front plate to protect the sniper's head from machine-gun, stray, armour-piercing or aimed bullets penetrating the sandbags immediately touching each side of the frontal or sniping plate.

The sniper could, of course, protect himself by building up several thicknesses of sandbags behind the plates, but by so doing his position becomes very cramped and uncomfortable, so whenever plates are available it is always best to use them.

All these dummy bags must conform to the appearance of the parapet and must not be filled with straw or hay, as this material soon loses its shape if subjected to light pressure. Old sandbags or rags make the best filling. The dummies must be filled very tightly, particularly the corners.

No. 2 Loophole.

This is very similar to No. 1 except that it is used in more uneven or broken parapets and the " choked " end of the sandbag is protruding.

The best position for this type of plate is on ground level or first row of bags, as in Fig. 2c.

If placed on ground level great care must be exercised by the sniper that the blast of discharge does not stir up a small cloud of sand or dust from the parapet and thereby give his position away to the enemy. To overcome this danger the sniper should soak a sandbag in water and just before daylight place it flat on the parapet in front of his loophole ; the outside edges of the sandbag should be cut into an uneven or jagged shape with a knife just to destroy the outline of the bag and make it blend with the parapet.

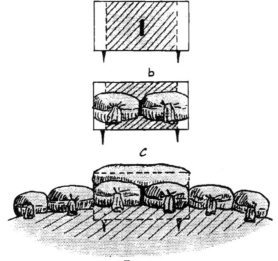

FIG. 2.

No. 3 Loophole.

This is called the Dummy Header Loophole, and can be used for sniping or observation. It is attached to a steel plate in a similar manner to Nos. 1 and 2.

Fig. 3c shows how the dummy is filled, first of all with a circular tin, and packed all round with pieces of rag or old sandbags.

A piece of invisible wire, usually thin black enamelled telephone wire (obtained from the Signalling Section), is fastened to the upper lip of the choke and a small weight sewn on the lip, which allows the choke to close and present a normal appearance when not in use.

Fig. 3d shows the dummy in position and choke closed.

Fig. 3b shows the choke open ready for business. As a matter of fact, in real practice the choke never appears so obviously open as in this diagram.

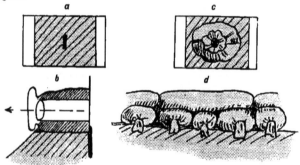

FIG. 3.

No. 4 Loophole.

Between two headers placed on ground level as in Fig. 4b, and used for sniping or observation. This is a very simple loophole to construct and a very effective one when completed, and most difficult to spot if carefully manipulated.

The choke end and a small portion of the neck of a sandbag is cut off and nailed to a small piece of board as in Fig. 4a. This is held in position by a stretcher sandbag as in Fig. 4b.

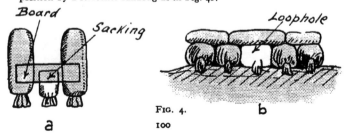

FIG. 4.

The loophole is opened and closed with invisible wire, a small weight being attached to the choke to make it fall into correct position.

No. 5 " Mouse Trap " Loophole.

This loophole is for use only in earth parapets, being placed in front of the loophole in a sniping plate as in Fig. 5c.

The movable wooden lid attached to the mouse trap is disguised by driving nails through it as in Fig. 5a, and if the parapet is of ordinary earth a small sod is cut out, and " stuck " on the nails, grass side downwards.

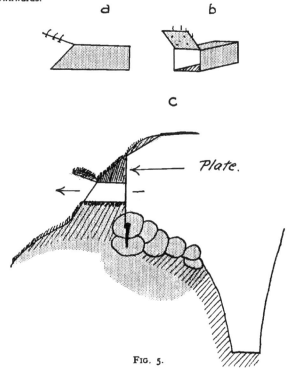

FIG. 5.

No. 6 Loophole with Plate turned Round.

A sniping plate was sometimes used in this position during the last war to enable snipers using rifles with telescopic sights offset to the left (as in the periscope prism mounting) to fire through the loophole.

All steel sniping plates issued during the war were of the same pattern, the aperture evidently being cut for open-sighted rifles, although aim could be taken with certain telescopic sights if mounted centrally and low. This loophole is disguised in a similar manner to No. 4.

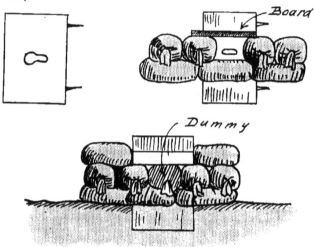

FIG. 6.

No. 7 Loophole for Telescopic Sights.

This loophole must be used only in the parados because, in order to give a wide field of view for diagonal or cross fire, it is undesirable to resort to a steel plate for protection. This loophole should only be used occasionally. The sniper can use it in the early morning or evening, fire one well-aimed shot and then move away to another position. A jagged hole is cut in the sacking in front of the aperture in the box. This is a simple loophole to construct and very difficult to spot.

FIG. 7.

It cannot be used in the parapet because stray bullets might come through at any moment and kill or wound men walking in the trench.

No. 8 Loophole.

Like No. 7, this type of loophole can be used only in the parados because it is not protected by a plate.

A sandbag shaped as in Fig. 8a is filled with broken brick, gravel or concrete and is pushed slightly forward or out of line with remainder of bags in parados in order to obtain enfilade fire.

Observation of this bag from the front reveals nothing ; everything looks quite symmetrical and in line as in Fig. 8b.

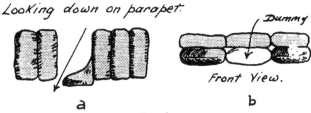

Looking down on parapet.

Front View.

a   b

FIG. 8.

No. 9 Observation Box.

This box can be used anywhere for purposes of front-line observation. It is very simple to construct and place in position, and was used with very good results by observers of the Canadian Corps when holding the Vimy front.

It can be used in sandbags, in grass, in earth, in chalk. It gives a wide field of vision, and is most difficult to detect.

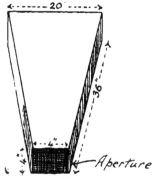

FIG. 9.

No. 10 Observation Loophole (Dummy Header).

This loophole should be constructed in the parados for observation, and is quite comfortably arranged as a sitting position as in Fig. 10b.

In Fig. 10a, when two-thirds of one side of a new sandbag is cut off the remainder of the " bag " part is filled with rags and an oval piece of board tacked into position behind the rags to hold them in place.

The dummy header is held in position as already described in No. 4 Loophole.

If manipulated carefully, a very wide field of view can be obtained and at the same time the observation post is invisible even with the most powerful telescope at 100 yards.

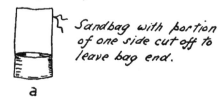

Sandbag with portion of one side cut off to leave bag end.

a

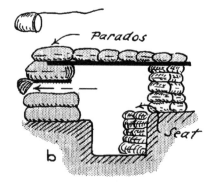

Parados

Seat

b

c

c

As the O.P. appears in parados.

Fig. 10.

No. 11 Box Loophole for Cross Fire.

This type of loophole was invented in order—

    (a) To obtain cross fire.

    (b) To disguise the actual aperture in the sniping plate.

    (c) To protect the sniper from a direct shot.

The possibility of an aimed shot coming in at a correct angle to enter the aperture in the plate is a very remote one.

The construction of this loophole should be practised behind the lines before any attempt is made to build it in a front-line parapet.

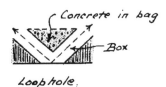

Loophole.

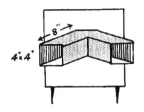

The two apertures are disguised with shutters of transparent gauze.

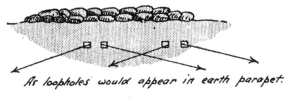

As loopholes would appear in earth parapet.

FIG. 11.

No. 12 Rum Jar Observation Post.

This is a very simple but effective method of observation not only for trained observers, but for sentries or any other man in the trenches when it is dangerous to look over the top of the parapet.

An ordinary sandbag with the bottom cut open is tied round a rum jar as shown in the diagram, the bottom of the rum jar having been removed.

FIG. 12.

No. 13 Old Boot Sniping Post.

This disguise can sometimes be used with good effect on an earth or chalk parapet where debris of all sorts has been thrown over and left to weather for some days.

About two-thirds of the sole of the boot is removed and the remainder of the boot is then placed over the aperture as shown in the diagram.

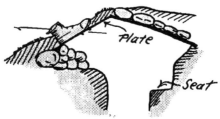

FIG. 13.

No. 14 Old Hat Sniping Post.

If an old service cap is placed in a position as shown in the following diagram and used as a disguise for sniping plate, it will be found very effective. An old weather-beaten hat is very difficult to detect with a good telescope at 200 yards when lying on a parapet.

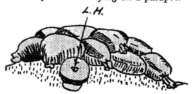

FIG. 14.

No. 15 Oblong Tin for Sniping on Observation.

This method of disguise is for use in chalk or earth parapets only. The oblong tin is placed in front of the aperture in a sniping plate and then built round with earth or chalk until it is flush with the parapet.

The lid of the box is painted with tar and, while wet, earth and gravel are thrown on it, in order to conform to the general appearance of the parapet.

The lid is pushed open from the inside and closed with a piece of wire which is attached to one cover of the lid.

It is safer to use this method for observation rather than sniping.

FIG. 15.

No. 16 Bent Sniping Plate.

This type of sniping plate was advocated in 1916 for use by snipers. It was not generally adopted, but a certain number were bent at Army workshops at the front to fill special orders.

The plates were far easier to place in position than the ordinary flat plates, easier to conceal, and bullets were more easily deflected.

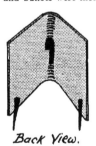

Back View.

FIG. 16.

Construction of Posts.

Points to remember.

Prone Position.

To be comfortable the prone position should always be excavated or constructed obliquely to the line of fire, as in Fig. 17a. Fig. 17b is the incorrect method.

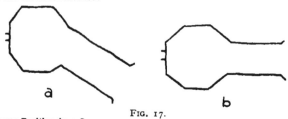

FIG. 17.

Prone Position in a Sap.

If it is necessary to drive out a sap under the parapet for a prone sniping post, the last six feet at least should be inclined upwards; this makes a great difference to the comfort of the position.

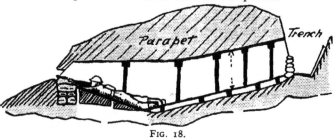

FIG. 18.

Sitting Position in Parapet.

Method of constructing a sitting position in parapet or parados.

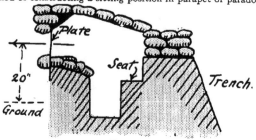

FIG. 19.

Head Space Construction.

A very common fault in the construction of sniping and observation posts is to build the overhead cover flat instead of providing head space by sloping the boards upwards from the plate, as in Fig. 20b.

It frequently happened during the last war that much time was spent and interest taken in the construction of certain sniping and observation posts, only to find when completed that the head cover was too flat and loophole too high up, so that when observing one's head was crammed tightly up against the roof when the telescope was in position. There is nothing more uncomfortable to the observer or sniper than this.

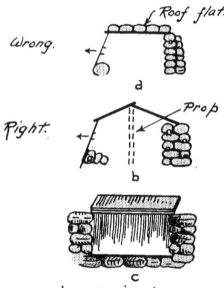

Front view showing head cover sloped upwards.

FIG. 20.

Snipers' Hides.

The following are diagrams of one of the most successful hides used during the last war for sniping from No Man's Land. If this type of hide is meant to be permanent it must never be built forward of our own wire or other entanglements. The usual procedure during the last war was to make the excavation near the outer edge of the wire, or in such position that German patrols would not be likely to spot it.

The siting of this type of hide depends a good deal on the possibilities to be obtained in the way of inflicting casualties on the enemy. It is not always essential to obtain a wide field of view. It can be built to command a special section of the enemy front if necessary. In one instance a hide was built in the forward edge of our wire to watch for a very aggressive German sniper who was operating, it was thought, at a range of about 180 yards, being the width of No Man's Land from parapet to parapet. It was before the days of artistic dummy heads and other camouflage, but a dummy head was made by stuffing a piece of sandbag and then painting a face on it; a Glengarry was then placed jauntily on top of this and the dummy carefully exposed over the parapet. No matter how crudely it was made, it had the desired effect of drawing fire on three occasions in two days. The direction of the first shot was obtained by the " strike " of the bullet on the parapet, and in the early morning of the third day our sniper in the hide (an officer) spotted the German sniper exposed to the shoulders between sandbags in the parapet and is certain he killed him.

In a very short time the German sniping was dominated almost entirely from this one hide, and the latter was never spotted.

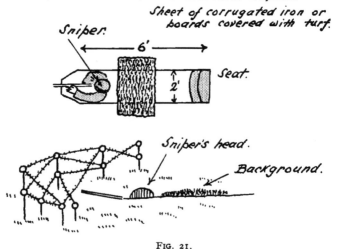

FIG. 21.

Posts in No Man's Land.

No hides or posts must be built or occupied in No Man's Land unless they are protected by wire or other good obstacle. It is obvious that patrols during the night would be certain to locate any post out in the open, and in due course the occupants would be captured or killed.

The only time that any prepared post can be occupied in No Man's Land, close to the enemy front line, is immediately before an attack taking place in daylight. This method was very successfully adopted by a sniper of the 29th Canadian Infantry Battalion. During the fighting on the Somme he dug in during the night within sixty yards of the German parapet, and in the early morning, when a company of the 29th advanced and was held up by machine-gun fire, he spotted the machine gun and, aiming carefully through the aperture, fired a shot, and the machine gun stopped. Again it opened, and after the second shot it stopped. Again it opened up, and with the third shot it stopped altogether. The company carried on with the advance and later, on entering the trench and examining the machine-gun post, they found two dead machine gunners and a bullet through the mechanism of the gun, which put it out of action.

Double Plate Loophole.

Fig. 22a and b will explain the construction of this sniping plate. This type of plate was said to have been used to some extent by the Guards Division on the Ypres front in 1916.

Although this plate enables the sniper to cover a wide front and provides an almost invulnerable protection against rifle fire, it is a very heavy and awkward device to carry about and also requires much care when being placed in position in the parapet or parados. A solid foundation is essential, otherwise its weight inclines it to tilt slightly forward or backwards, thereby destroying the field of fire.

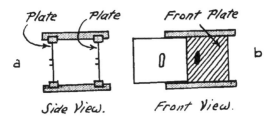

FIG. 22.

The Kidney or Universal Loophole.

The aperture in the plate in Fig. 23*a* was designed by a Canadian officer at the 2nd Army Sniping School in 1916 for general use in preference to the ordinary aperture as in Fig. 23*b*, which precludes the convenient use of telescopic sights mounted centrally and is altogether useless if telescopic sights are offset.

The " Kidney " loophole was designed to take any telescopic sight, whether offset or mounted centrally. If open sights were to be used, the size of the aperture could be conveniently regulated by means of a small steel shutter.

Sniping plates or snipers' plates, as the name implies, were originally made to be used by snipers. In spite of this fact and the knowledge that the original aperture was more or less useless for telescopic sights, which knowledge was imparted from many fighting units on the Western Front, the old pattern was still adhered to until the end. In a few special cases the Army workshops at the front were able to turn out the new type of plate. The First Army workshop made a hundred of these plates for the Canadian Corps.

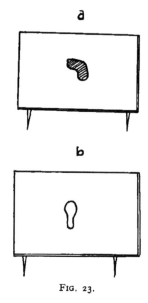

Fig. 23.

Examples of the Use of Portable Armoured Observation Posts in Trenches for Sentries.

Gauze

FIG. 24.—ARMOURED SANDBAG OBSERVATION POST.

FIG. 25.—HOOD OF PAINTED TRANSPARENT CANVAS USED FOR SCOUTS OR LOOKING OVER PARAPETS.

Gauze

FIG. 26.—ARMOURED TURF OBSERVATION POST.

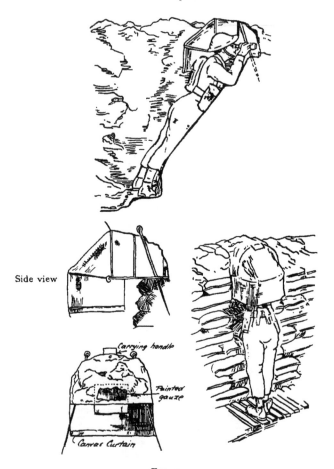

Side view

Carrying handle

Painted gauze

Canvas Curtain

FIG. 27.

DUTIES OF BATTALION INTELLIGENCE OFFICER

The Battalion Intelligence Officer should always undertake, in addition to his ordinary duties, the duty of Scouting, Sniping and Observation Officer to his unit.

The present organization according to War Establishment is as follows :—

Intelligence	1 Officer.	
	1 N.C.O.	
	6 O.Rs.	
Snipers	8 N.C.Os. or Guardsmen (these should be chosen from companies, and attached to H.Q. for operations and training).	

Each rifle company will be responsible for supplying two snipers, and will be responsible for replacing their own in the event of casualties.

The eight battalion snipers will not form part of the Intelligence Section, but will work under the orders of the Intelligence Officer. As their name implies, they will be trained as expert scouts, observers and snipers, and will also be well grounded in map reading and intelligence duties.

NOTE.—Snipers are valuable men and take time to train ; therefore all tasks other than those directly connected with their duties as scouts, observers and snipers should be assigned to them with great discretion.

To supplement this organization, it is essential that one should endeavour to have at least two trained scouts or snipers per platoon in rifle companies ; that is to say, there should always be a reserve of twenty-four trained scout-snipers capable of replacing any wastage of personnel in the battalion sniping or intelligence unit.

It will be the duty of the Intelligence Officer, his N.C.O. and other ranks to train these additional platoon scouts.

1. Transport.

War Establishment :

In 8-cwt. truck (second-in-command), I.O. plus 2 O.Rs.

Motor-cycle, 1 N.C.O. (Intelligence).

Bicycles, 3 O.Rs.

NOTE.—War Establishment provides for—

1 Motor-cycle, Regimental Police N.C.O.

3 Motor-cycles, Regimental Police 3 O.Rs.

These could be under the Intelligence Officer, or their bicycles might be handed over to the Battalion Intelligence Section, when circumstances permit.

In any war of movement, the Battalion Intelligence Officer **must** have a car or truck of his own, and he must make every endeavour to provide himself with one.

2. Duties of the Battalion Intelligence Section during the Approach March.

(*a*) On occasions it may be necessary for the Intelligence Section to carry out a reconnaissance of the route to be followed by the battalion. To do this a thorough training in the compiling of Route Reports should be carried out. This requires a thorough knowledge of map reading, knowledge of gradients, means of ascertaining strength of bridges and preparation of Route Reports.

(*b*) When the battalion is on the move by day or by night, on foot or lifted, it may devolve on the Intelligence Section to assist in traffic control and intercommunication.

All Intelligence personnel should therefore be able to ride a motorcycle. For controlling traffic at night, all Intelligence personnel should be provided with torches with blue bulbs.

(*c*) On contact being gained by day, one group (three other ranks) should be sent on to each of the forward companies to report to the Company Commander and then to establish an observation post. Any information should be transmitted to Battalion H.Q. at once, Company H.Q. being informed at the same time.

3. Organization at Battalion H.Q. during the Approach March and Contact Stage.

(*a*) A copy of every message should be shown to the Intelligence Officer or Sergeant.

(*b*) Incoming messages not through signals, but from Intelligence observation posts, should come direct to the Intelligence Officer. If important, he should then show them to the Commanding Officer.

(*c*) On taking up positions, Company Commanders should send in to the Intelligence Officer a field sketch or map enlargement showing positions, fixed lines, Company H.Q., etc. The Intelligence Officer should see that this is done.

(*d*) An Intelligence map showing own positions and any enemy positions located should be produced as soon as possible, and it should be available for any officer to see.

(*e*) Situation reports should be sent to Brigade H.Q. at stated times, usually at dawn and dusk, and anything vital should be sent through at once.

(*f*) An observation post within easy reach of Battalion H.Q. can almost always be obtained and is of extreme importance. This could be connected by line with Battalion H.Q.

4. Equipment.

The present establishment of equipment leaves much to be desired. The **ideal** scale of equipment would be as follows :—

Transport   Intelligence Officer   ⎫   1 8-cwt. truck.
                1 N.C.O.   ⎬   7 motor-cycles.
                6 O.Rs.   ⎭

Each member of Intelligence Section should be equipped with—

1 Stalking telescope   ⎫   These may be used in conjunction
1 oil compass   ⎬   with the snipers, who may be
1 map case   ⎭   made responsible for them.

1 torch (blue bulb)   ...   For traffic control.

1 pair of binoculars

The Intelligence Section should possess a large box which should be capable of carrying—

8 stalking telescopes   ...   These should always be carried on the man when possible.

1 periscope

Intelligence box   ...   This is a flat box. It should contain coloured pine, chinagraph pencils, protractor, dividers, maps of the area, a torch, pencils and message pads.

Six files   ...   (1) In ; (2) Out ; (3) Daily Intelligence Reports ; (4) Air photographs ; (5) spare ; (6) spare.

War Diary.

The snipers should have a box capable of carrying an assortment of camouflage robes.

This should also be large enough to carry eight telescopic sights (though these, whenever possible, should be carried on the man).

Some Duties of the Intelligence Officer in the Line in Trench Warfare.

1. It will be found difficult actually to supervise the whole of the snipers and scouts, but the sixteen and as many of the " picked scouts " of the sections as may be necessary to man his various posts should be under his immediate control.

2. It is his job to select, construct (or see that they are constructed), organize and utilize the battalion sniping and observation posts.

3. His duties will include the warning and arranging of any patrols that are required and, by virtue of constant patrolling, No Man's Land on his battalion front should become his property.

4. He must collect and sift all information from—

      (a) Companies in the line,

      (b) Observation posts,

      (c) Snipers,

      (d) Patrols.

5. From the above he should compile the Battalion Daily Intelligence Report or Summary, and in doing this must use tact in correcting, or amplifying, or in " washing out " obviously dud reports. He must keep the log book of his sector, and keep up to date the Intelligence maps of the sector.

6. He must properly organize and control the observation and sniping of the whole battalion sector, keeping close touch with flanking units, and should construct " Rayboards " for spotting areas under bombardment.

Some Duties of the Battalion Intelligence Officer in Rest and Reserve.

1. He must re-zero and examine telescopic and open-sighted rifles belonging to each man in his command.

2. He must arrange for the training of both old and new personnel.

3. He must arrange, if possible, that the sixteen Intelligence personnel and snipers proper be billeted together and use them to assist with the instruction of the platoon scouts.

4. He must cultivate a liaison with all Company Commanders, and endeavour to make the whole battalion keen on Intelligence work by lectures and the getting of good results—results which in the line save life and give Company Commanders detailed information of their front.

5. He must reorganize and re-equip his command before going back into the line and, together with his N.C.Os., thoroughly reconnoitre the line before relief takes place.

Some Duties of the Battalion Intelligence Officer in Open Warfare.

1. It will obviously be impossible for him to keep the whole of the scouts, observers and snipers under his control.

2. His own position will depend entirely upon the formation of the ground and the general situation.

3. His chief job is to form an unfailing channel of communication between front-line Battalion and Brigade H.Q.

4. He should know the Attack Scheme backwards, and previously organize a sound scheme of " Battle Intelligence and Observation."

5. He must sift and forward to Brigade H.Q. all reports.

The following diagram shows a very efficient scheme of " Battle Intelligence."

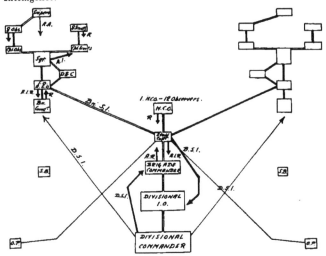

FRONT-LINE INTELLIGENCE SYSTEM.

I.O.	...	Intelligence Officer.
D.S.I.	...	Divisional Summary of Intelligence.
Bn. S.I.	...	Battalion Summary of Intelligence.
A.I.	...	Advice and Information.
A.S.O.	...	Assistant Scout Officer.
D. & C.	...	Draughtsman and Clerk.
S.B.	...	Support Battalion.
R.	...	Reports.
B.S.I.	...	Brigade Summary of Intelligence.

Generally.

1. He forms liaison between front line and Battalion H.Q.

2. He should be *au fait* with the general situation and with details of his own and the enemy sector.

3. He should make himself the map and aeroplane photograph expert of his battalion.

4. He should be responsible for " Front Line Observation " from our line to the German reserve line.

5. He should generally be responsible for the upkeep of his command as an efficient, fully organized fighting unit.

Notes on Reports.

1. They should be concise, though containing all information calculated to be of the slightest use.

2. They must clearly indicate the degree of accuracy with which they are made and the amount of reliance that can be placed on them. A surmise or deduction must be reported as such.

3. Personal impressions and conclusions should be given as this often starts a correct train of thought which would not otherwise have occurred to the reader.

4. They should be tabulated, names should be in block capitals, and a copy should always be sent.

5. The actual form of report varies in battalions and brigades, but the headings given in the Section on "Intelligence Logs or Reports" are fairly general.

6. Information published in official summaries should always reach the individual in the front line who was responsible for obtaining it. In this way the red-hot keenness essential to success in this work will be kept alive.

7. He should be the Battalion Commander's right-hand man and constant companion when in the line ; he goes with him everywhere, and takes notes for letters and orders to be given.

Co-operation within the Section.

This should come within the province of the Battalion Intelligence Officer.

1. Co-operation between snipers and scouts not only when on duty, but when in billets, is most important.

2. They should work together whenever the occasion presents itself.

3. There should be co-operation with snipers in battalions on either flank.

4. It is most important for Intelligence and Scout Officers to co-operate with similar officers of battalions on flanks.

5. Men in the front line outside the Intelligence Section should be asked to impart any information which it might be important for the snipers, observers or scouts to know.

RELIEFS.

Indications of Reliefs and Withdrawals of Enemy's Units.

It is highly important that not only should prompt information be secured of any change of enemy units, but that new units be quickly identified.

In order to detect changes in the form of reliefs or complete withdrawals of enemy's units from the front line, the following outline of indications may be useful for the guidance and information of observers, especially in the front-line system :—

1. Activity of Front-Line Fire, etc.

Uniform increase of rifle and machine-gun fire may indicate either—

(a) A covering for a relief in progress.

(b) The characteristics of a new unit, which may be more aggressive or perhaps more nervous.

2. Increase of Trench-Mortar Fire and Bombing.

In trench mortars it may mean new registration or the employment of these instead of artillery, which may have been withdrawn or be saving ammunition.

Bombing without apparent cause, especially into No Man's Land at night, may indicate a new unit of nervous characteristics. Frequent cases of enemy bombing his own wire have been reported.

3. Increase in Flares.

Increase in the number of flares sent up by enemy along a battalion front (not locally) will, other things being equal, usually indicate a relief, either—

(a) To cover a movement of relief already on ;

(b) As characteristic of a new unit, unacquainted with the locality and possibly nervous.

Note.—Conversely, the decrease in fire, bombing, flares, etc., may indicate a new unit of quieter characteristics, or purposely quiet to avoid retaliation, particularly if the unit has been recently in severe fighting and wants a quiet time.

Activity of Movement.

Increase of patrols in front of enemy's wire may indicate a new unit either—

(a) By aggressiveness in keeping patrol contact ; or

(b) By covering the operations of a unit particularly active in working parties on front line.

Increase of railway, tramway and transport activity, if detected, is a pretty safe guide to spotting a relief.

Often the direction of the movement can be seen or heard and, depending upon the time of day or night, the movement in or out can be summarized.

Activity of Working Parties.

It is difficult to deduce the presence of a new unit by its activity in working unless by comparison with its predecessor as to method, size of parties, etc. The locality in which work is being done may or may not indicate a new unit.

The relief of a unit from the front is generally accompanied by a cessation of working parties for at least one night whilst getting settled down ; this can only be detected by continuous observation both before and after.

Noise on Front Line and Approaches.

A close study of noises coming from enemy's trenches as discovered by patrols will usually indicate the nature of movement. Experienced observers will frequently be able to recognize the noise made by an ordinary relief.

A relief by troops new to a locality will invariably be noisier than by those accustomed to the trenches.

Listening posts or listening scouts are often of the greatest value and should not be discontinued.

Appearance of New Troops.

Observers frequently send in reports indicating new types of uniform in the trenches, usually of different colour—blue (Labour Battalion), green (Jaeger), etc. It is not likely that new troops can be safely detected by this means. All uniforms of fighting units are so nearly alike nowadays and fade readily or are dusty or muddy.

The actions of new troops, however, are often indicative of their ignorance of the locality. They will make more frequent use of periscopes and will oftentimes show their heads over the parapet more than older units.

Activity of Mining.

Officers carrying out Intelligence duties around the front line should consult Mining Officers in their trench areas as to indications of increased or decreased mining operations, which will oftentimes give a lead as to changes in units.

Activity of Artillery.

Enemy's artillery (such as divisional) in the course of reliefs will either wholly change, gradually by localities, or will change personnel only. In either case there is sure to be some cessation and some erratic operation.

In either case there also will be re-registration and more or less practice in putting down barrages, etc., both of which can be readily detected if the targets and nature of practice be closely observed.

The deductions to be made from the nature of guns and projectiles are technical and based on a large acquaintance with the enemy's projectiles.

Retirements.

Retirements have generally been carried out by the enemy between 0300 and 0500. Previous indications have been given by fires and explosions. An unusual number of Very lights has often shown when withdrawal was being effected.

Artillery fire has usually increased before withdrawal commenced, presumably to use up the ammunition with the gun.

NOTES ON GERMAN MILITARY ORGANIZATION.

Infantry.
A German infantry regiment is the equivalent of a British Brigade.

Command.
Under normal circumstances, a regiment is commanded by a Lieutenant-Colonel or a Colonel, a battalion by a Major, and a company by a Captain.

Organization.

The nominal roll of a—				Officers.	Other Ranks.
Regiment is	...	...	...	89	2,886
Battalion	...	...	...	23	777
M.G. Company ...		...	...	4	139

A battalion (ordinary) consists of—

> Headquarters,
> Signal Section,
> Three rifle companies,
> One machine-gun Company.

Lights.
Flares. To show the position of the leading infantry.
Very pistols. Four : Red, white, green and yellow lights.

Bivouacs.
Each infantryman has a camouflaged coloured waterproof sheet complete with poles, pegs and cords. A number of these can be fastened together to make improvised shelters or tents.

Pistol.
The pistol is the 1908 pattern, known as Pistole '08. The calibre is ·9 cm. (·351 in.), and its weight is 1 lb. 14¼ oz. It is semi-automatic. The magazine holds eight cartridges.

Machine Pistol.
A machine pistol 28/11 is carried by armoured cars and tanks as a subsidiary hand weapon. Its calibre is ·885 cm. (·35 in.), with effective range of 300 ft. as automatic and 1,000 ft. when firing single shots. Feed is by band magazine holding either 50, 32 or 20 rounds. Rate of sustained fire is 250 rounds per minute.

Grenade.
The hand grenade is the same pattern as used in the last war, 1914-18. It weighs 1 lb. 5¼ oz., and consists of a cylindrical sheet-iron head containing explosives, mounted on a hollow wooden handle through which a friction wire runs. The maximum range is about 40 yds., and the danger zone extends to a radius of 20 yds. The heads may be disconnected from the handles and tied in a bunch of six round the head of a seventh grenade for throwing against tanks or other obstacles.

Staff Distinctions.

In field service order the main distinguishing marks of the staff are—
On the trousers ... ... Two broad crimson stripes.

Sword Knots.

The sword knots and bayonet knots of lance-corporals and privates show by their colour the battalion and company to which the wearer belongs.

Training Manuals.

German training manuals show the importance of—
Speed.
Surprise.
Mobility.
Early information obtained by contact on which the Commander can base his plan.
Use of darkness.
Deception.

National Crest and Badges.

The regimental crests and badges of the type worn by the British Army are replaced by the National Badge and the National Rosette and the National Colours.

Number of Regiment or Equivalent Unit.

This is worn on the centre of the shoulder strap.

Defence—Concealment and Camouflage.

Considerable emphasis is laid on concealment and camouflage, which the Germans treat as one and the same subject.

They define it as an attempt to adapt oneself so closely both in shape and colour to one's surroundings, as to be concealed from the enemy, or to render observation difficult for him.

According to the German theory, camouflage is divided into two parts—

(a) That part which is regulated by the Higher Command and for which instructions appear in Orders.

(b) That part which concerns the individual soldier and which the latter carries out on his own initiative, without waiting for orders.

Concealment.

Concealment is regarded as being so important that it is even suggested in the regulations that it may be preferable to use less favourable ground, if by so doing the intentions and organization of the defence are less clear to the enemy than would be the case if a more obviously favourable position were selected.

HANDLING OF PRISONERS

Important Identification and Documents.

Regimental Identifications (German).

1. Identity Disc.—A copy of the marks on the identity disc ; this disc must not be taken from prisoners. This is the surest method of identifying a man's unit. The upper half gives the man's name, address, date of birth, regiment, battalion, company and his regimental number at the depot. On the lower half are the numbers of the regiment, battalion and company to which the man was posted, and his regimental number.

If a man is transferred from one unit to another, the old markings are struck out and new particulars added, but not the orginal markings of the depot unit.

SPECIMEN.

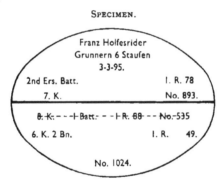

The above specimen shows—

    (a) The soldier's full name.

    (b) Place and date of birth.

    (c) That he joined the 2nd Ersatz Battalion, Infantry Regiment No. 78, 7th Company.

    (d) That his number at the depot was 893.

    (e) That he was thereafter posted to the 6th Company, 2nd Battalion, Infantry Regiment No. 49, his number being 1024.

A new form of disc was issued during the latter period of the last war ; it was perforated along the centre. The depot particulars were marked on each half of one side, and subsequent postings on each half of reverse side. If the owner is killed the lower half is broken off and returned to Germany, the upper half being buried with the body.

2. The Pay Book.—The pay book with brown paper cover, usually found in the coat tail pocket, must not be taken from prisoners, but may be taken from the dead.

3. Markings.—The shoulder strap is marked with the regimental number or monogram. It should be stated whether it is taken from a tunic or greatcoat.

The number of the regiment is marked on the inside of the flap of the cartridge pouch and also on the bayonet near the hilt. It is also stencilled on the tunic lining and inside the cap.

Handling of Prisoners.

The handling of prisoners will be discussed later from the interrogation point of view. It is necessary, however, to give here more complete details of the system employed in the Great War up to and including open warfare.

Prisoners and documents should be sent to the place where the preliminary examination is to take place with the least possible delay. Their documents will be forwarded with them to Brigade or Divisional H.Q., where the Divisional Intelligence Officer will carry out the preliminary examination.

The Divisional Intelligence Officer will telegraph or telephone to Corps as early as possible, informing them of the units to which the prisoners belong, the order of battle, and any information of immediate tactical importance.

The Divisional Intelligence Officer will also glance through documents to obtain any information of immediate importance, and send them to Corps as soon as possible.

Battalion Procedure.

A German-speaking other rank was stationed at the battalion collecting-point. Officers were searched here for documents (if this had not already been done), these documents being placed in separate sandbags and forwarded with them to the divisional cage.

Two German-speaking other ranks sorted prisoners by companies and sent back representatives of every unit immediately they came in. If prisoners of the same unit were captured later in the day, they were sent back as if they belonged to a new unit.

It was pointed out to all concerned that it is of the utmost tactical importance that representatives of all units (10 per cent.) be sent back immediately, including N.C.Os., runners, signallers, and all specialists.

The German-speaking other ranks at battalion collecting posts sent with each batch of prisoners a list of their units, and periodically a rough estimate of the number of prisoners of each unit retained for stretcher-bearers, etc.

Divisional Prisoners' Cage.

Divisional Intelligence Officers selected the prisoners they required for examination and sent the remainder to the Corps cage immediately.

N.C.Os. should be searched at the divisional cage and their documents forwarded with them to the Corps cage.

Other ranks will be searched at Corps cage. Sufficient prisoners should be sent back at once from battalion collecting-points to enable Intelligence Officers to retain those they require and still to send on at once to Corps cage representative prisoners of all units.

The usual procedure was for divisions to instruct battalions through brigades how many prisoners per unit were required to be sent back at once.

DIAGRAM ILLUSTRATING METHOD OF HANDLING PRISONERS IN OPEN WARFARE.

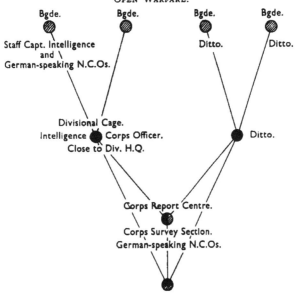

Advanced Corps Cage

This chart outlines the general guiding principles and arrangements for divisional prisoners-of-war collecting posts and Corps cage.

During the initial phases of an attack in open warfare the following information only is necessary from prisoners :—

    (a) Identification, battalion, regiment, division, vicinity captured.
    (b) Captured documents, enemy defensive lines, dispositions, H.Q. boundaries.
    (c) Summarized contents of messages, documents or orders *re* troops in rear area.

Selected prisoners or prisoner to be sent back for special examination.

If a Soldier is captured.

All the information a soldier need supply to the enemy is his name and rank, nothing more. On no account should he allow himself to be drawn into any discussion.

Prisoners may find themselves in a cage, cell or room in company probably with an enemy dressed in British uniform and speaking perfect English, and to all appearances a prisoner himself, so that unless prisoners are on their guard they may unknowingly give away valuable information.

The same procedure has happened continually in military clearing stations and hospitals where selected enemy spies have been camouflaged as wounded British soldiers for the purposes of obtaining information.

Be on your guard for the first few days at least, particularly so if one happens to have been on any H.Q. Staff or any specialist section. Great efforts will be made to obtain information from officers or men of this description.

Most valuable information has at times been given to the enemy by our prisoners, and it has been proved on one or two occasions that the information was obtained entirely by camouflaged methods, to the intense astonishment of the man when he was confronted with what he had done on being at a later date repatriated or having escaped.

A man who willingly supplies the enemy with information is a traitor to his country and should be shot.

The best advice is—

SAY NOTHING !

INTELLIGENCE LOGS OR REPORTS

There are four reports or intelligence logs which particularly concern the Sniping and Intelligence Sections. They are :—

> The Daily Report or Intelligence Log.
> The Patrol Report or Summary.
> The Daily Summary of Intelligence.
> The Handing Over Report.

The Daily Reports or Logs.

1. These reports are a summary of the notes which should be prepared by each sniper, observer or scout or the Scout Section every time he or they come off duty in the front line.

2. If any post is occupied by two or more men they should **each** sign the report or log.

3. These reports should be collected at specified times by the N.C.O. on duty, who will condense them or summarize them and hand them to the Intelligence Officer.

Observer's Notes or Log.—Written in a Log Book provided for the purpose, which should be left in the observation post. A carbon copy should be prepared of all messages sent in and the carbon copy handed over on relief. If possible sketch of enemy position should accompany this log.

OBSERVER'S INTELLIGENCE LOG.

Post 1.

Tour of Duty : 0800—1600 hrs.   25 Nov. 18.

Time.	Remarks.	Action taken. Deductions.
0800—0830	Quiet.	
0900—0930	77s. front line vicinity ACHEVILLE ROAD.	
0930—1000	T.Ms. front line vicinity ACHEVILLE ROAD.	
1000—1045	Shelling Quarries with A.Is.	
		J. Shaw, *Observer.*

At 1600 hrs. or thereabouts the Observers' Notes are collected by the N.C.O. in charge of the Observers and rewritten as follows :—

OBSERVATION REPORT OR LOG.

To : I.O.

Posts Nos. 1, 2, 3.
0730—1730 hrs.
25 Nov. 18.

Enemy Activity.	
Artillery.	Artillery a little more active than usual all day. In the evening enemy put over several prolonged bursts heavy guns, principally on front line.
T.Ms.	Very quiet—few bursts early morning and again in evening.
Aircraft.	Nil.
Our Activity.	
Artillery.	Very quiet all day.
M.Gs.	A few bursts during day.
T.Ms.	Active on front line.
Aircraft.	Usual patrolling.
General.	

(*Signed*) H. HARRISON, *Cpl.*,
Bn. Observer.

Sniper's Notes or Intelligence Logs.—Same procedure as Observer's. Notes collected at specified times.

SNIPER'S NOTES OR LOG.

Post 1.

To : I.O.
Tour of Duty : 0800—1600 hrs.

Date.
25 Nov. 18.

Time.	
0830	No movement visible.
0835	Shot at man coming down communication trench. Visible for a few yards. Result, not observed.
0950	No movement.
1000	Two hours observing carefully over parapet right flank of the front line. Hit claimed here T.16.6.
1600	No further movement observed.

T. DIXON,
Sniper.

SNIPING REPORT.

To : I.O.

22 Feb. 40.

Enemy Sniping.	A few shots fired on our right front ; no casualties. Not aggressive.
Our Sniping.	Visibility bad in early morning and again in afternoon. A few targets engaged in BULL RING. One hit observed at T.16.6.

(*Signed*) J. HARRISON, *Cpl.*

NIGHT OBSERVER'S LOG.

Post 3.

To : I.O.   Night 13/14 Feb. 40.

Tour of Duty : 1600—0700 hrs.

Time.	
1700—1800	Very quiet ; 4 L.T.Ms. on right battalion front.
1800—1830	Very quiet.
1830—1900	Bursts of enemy M.G. fire along whole front.
1900—2000	Battery in front of O.P. fired 35 rounds.
2100—2130	Many white flares sent up by enemy.
2130—2200	Red and green light flares sent up by enemy.

(Signed) J. SMITH,
Night Observer.

NIGHT OBSERVATION REPORT.

Posts 3 & 4.

To : I.O.   Night 13/14 Feb. 40.

Enemy Activity.

Artillery.	Not very active, 35 4.1's being fired all night.
T.Ms.	Very quiet.
M.Gs.	Fairly active all night firing short bursts.
Flares	Usual white.

Our Activity.

Artillery.	Very active all night ; approx. 250 rounds fired by battery near O.P.
M.Gs.	Usual amount of harassing fire.
Night Bombing.	Nil.

P. LAMB, *Cpl.,*
Bn. Observer.

The Patrol Report.

This report is made out by the Scout Officer and handed to the Intelligence Officer, who then prepares what is usually called the Patrol Report. Some Intelligence Officers call it the " Summary of Intelligence or Patrol Report." It makes very little difference. It is included in the summary of all reports to be handed in to the Battalion Commander by the Intelligence Officer at a specified time every morning.

PATROL REPORT AND SUMMARY.

............Regt.   0430—0600 hrs,

To : 2nd Brigade.   13 Feb. 40—14 Feb. 40.
            Ref. Map.

Enemy Activity.

Artillery.	Less active than usual. Only a few 5.9's scattered over front area.
T.Ms.	Normal. About 20 medium T.Ms. on " TOT " trenches.
M.Gs.	Quiet. Occasional bursts throughout night.
General Flares.	White flares—appear nervous.
Gas.	About 20 gas shells at 0525 on T.16.6.

Our Activity.

Artillery.	Our 18-pounders fairly active during night on enemy front line and support.
M.Gs.	Usual harassing fire.
Patrols.	A patrol of Lieut. Swan and 4 O.Rs. left our front line at 2200 and worked along outside our wire towards our left flank. This patrol came in at midnight and reported enemy wire to be in fairly good condition except in a few places. No enemy patrols were encountered and nothing unusual to report.

Wind E. Very mild. Gas alert.

J. BURNS, I.O.

For O.C................Bn.

When the report has been sent on to Brigade, the Intelligence Officer breathes a sigh of relief and has time probably to wash himself and find out if the Commanding Officer wants anything in particular, takes a walk round observation posts and sniper posts, visits Company Commander and others, makes inquiries as to maps and photos required, and discusses patrol work with Scout Officer and compares maps.

THE DAILY SUMMARY OF INTELLIGENCE
OR
INTELLIGENCE OFFICER'S REPORT.

Procedure.

The Intelligence Officer will collect all reports from his men, together with information from front, support and reserve trenches and Company Commanders ; also add any information he may have obtained himself when on patrol. He must keep eyes and ears open continuously.

Having obtained all possible information, he will hurry off to his dugout and summarize all information he has collected. That is, he will " comb out " the reports and separate **Definite** from **Indefinite** and condense the report as much as possible whenever it has not been done for him.

When his summary is completed the usual procedure is to get the Orderly Room Sergeant to type it at Battalion H.Q., then, in the absence of the Commanding Officer, take it to the Adjutant, who examines it and if it is correct hands it back to the Intelligence Officer for signature, after which it is sent to Brigade H.Q. at an appointed time.

At Brigade H.Q. it is examined by the Staff Captain Intelligence together with other summaries from battalions on right or left, and is still further condensed and sent to Division H.Q., where the same process is carried out ; it is then sent to Corps H.Q., where it remains for the time being until supplemented by news from the Army front, and the **Corps Summary,** as it is now called, is then issued to divisions, brigades and battalions—usually arriving at battalions about noon the next day.

It is prepared as follows :—

INTELLIGENCE OFFICER'S REPORT.

DAILY SUMMARY OF INTELLIGENCE.
10TH BN.

To 3rd Brig. H.Q.	*From* 0600 *to* 1930
Ref. Local Map.	20 *May* 40.

Enemy Activity.

Art.	During the day enemy put over 200 rds. of 77s. along TOAST—TOTNES—and front line.
T.Ms.	A few light T.Ms. on left Coy. frontage.
Wire.	Light T.Ms. operating on wire in vicinity of T.17a.
M.Gs.	Quiet.
Sniping.	Nil.
Aircraft.	None observed.
Movement.	Very little individual movement observed during day owing to poor visibility.

Our Activity.

Art.	A number of 18 pdrs. fired, landing in vicinity of OCHEVILLE and in rear.
T.Ms.	About 60 rds. on suspected M.G. emplacement at T.11a.
M.Gs.	Nil.
Sniping.	One hit observed at T.15a.
Aircraft.	Nil.
Visibility.	Poor.

A. LAWRENCE, *Lt.*,
B.I.O.,
For O.C. 10th Bn.

Intelligence Summaries.

Try to save unnecessary repetition in writing and thereby save time. The Intelligence Officer is always working against time in the front line.

Formula.

Try to use a short, clear, workable formula for your Intelligence Summary. Most brigades have a set formula; if so, you must abide by it.

HANDING-OVER REPORT AND WORKING MAPS.

Handing-Over Report.

This report should contain a summary of all the Intelligence collected during one tour of duty in the front line, maybe one, two or three days or more.

Handing-Over Reports should be exchanged between Intelligence Officer, N.C.O. and men, and should be each addressed as follows :—

Outgoing Officer to Taking-Over Officer.

HANDING-OVER REPORT.

15TH BATTALION.

To Relieving I.O.   *Apr.* 40.

4 to 9 incl.

FORMULA FOR HANDING-OVER REPORT.

Eight Heads.
1. General Activity of Enemy regarding :
    Rifle fire and sniping.
    M.G. fire.
    Artillery fire.
    Trench mortars.
    Lights.
    Bombs and rifle grenades.
    General attitude of enemy.
    Smoke.

2. Works.
    Working parties.
    Trenches.
    Dugouts.
    Wire.
    Emplacements.
    Listening posts.
    Saps.
    Mines.
    Trench trams.
    Loopholes.
    Dangerous places in our lines.

134

3. Roads.

4. Aircraft.

5. Identification.

6. Weather.

7. General.

8. Patrols.

The above eight marginal headings should be sufficient for any summary, although I have seen as many as thirty-three.

This same formula could also be used by Company Officers in front line when handing their reports to the Intelligence Officer.

Thorough liaison between outgoing and incoming troops is most imperative ; particularly is this so in sniping, observing and scouting.

Without thorough liaison there can be no continuity of observation and sniping, thereby causing much loss of information and possibly many casualties.

Whenever there was a break in this continuity of observation, sniping and patrolling, the Germans were very quick to take advantage of it ; their snipers and scouts immediately became very aggressive, and it was some time before they could be subdued again.

The following are a few faults to guard against in order to maintain efficient liaison :—

(a) Faulty or no Handing-Over Report.

(b) No trained snipers.

(c) No trained observers and scouts.

(d) Untrained or no Intelligence Officers or Scout Officers.

The usual fault was the absence of a Handing-Over Report.

The enemy must be kept continually under observation and sniping. There must be no break—the relieving battalion must be given all possible information.

Working Map.

Every Handing-Over Report should be accompanied by a working map, or situation map, drawn either roughly or correctly to scale. This map should be prepared at Brigade H.Q. by brigade draughtsmen ; on this map should be placed correctly and to scale the enemy trenches in front of the brigade sector.

The location of the trenches can be taken from aeroplane photos.

The working map should be drawn to a scale of 1/5,000 if possible ; if not, 1/10,000.

It is most important for snipers and observers to have a map of this sort ; they then take a far greater interest in their work and, besides, their references will be far more reliable.

If these maps are not procurable at Brigade H.Q., the Intelligence Officer should make enlargements of trench maps himself.

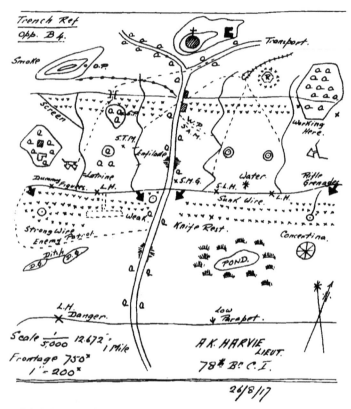

Trench Ref Opp. B 4.

Smoke

Screen

Transport.

O.P.

S.T.M.

Enfilade

Dummy Figures.

Clothing

L.H.

Weak.

Strong Wire

Enemy

Patrol

Ditch

P.8. P.8.

L.H.

Danger.

S.M.G.

S.L.H.

Water.

Sunk Wire.

Knife Rest.

L.H.

POND.

low

Parapet.

Working Here.

Rifle Grenades.

Concentina.

Scale 1/5,000 12.672" 1 Mile

Frontage 750ˣ

1" = 200ˣ

A.K. HARVIE
LIEUT.
78ᵗʰ Bⁿ C.I.

26/8/17

Points to remember when Mapping.

1. The position of the enemy governs all military maps.

2. The enemy right is always our left (positional warfare).

3. The North point has nothing to do with their position.

4. To avoid any danger of misunderstanding great care must be observed when signing one's name to a map and placing the scale, otherwise there may be some danger (particularly if the recipient of the map is new to the locality) of the enemy's position being taken as our own.

5. Details of our own position, trenches, dugouts, dumps, etc., should never be marked on any map which is to be taken into the front line. If it is found that the line we are taking over has been so damaged by shell fire that in certain places our own men would be exposed to the enemy snipers, then these spots should be marked on the maps until the necessary repairs have been completed.

6. If the enemy had obviously discovered any of our sniping or observation posts, these should be abandoned and marked as dangerous.

When forwarding Maps.

1. When forwarding maps for inspection be sure they are signed, the signature to be in the lower right-hand corner.

2. Either a correct or approximately correct scale should be used, such as—

> R.F. 1/5,000 ; 12·672 = 1 mile.
>
> or Frontage about 750 yds.
>
> or 1 in. = 200 yds., etc.

This scale should be placed in the lower left-hand corner.

3. In the upper left-hand corner should be written the Trench Reference in order to identify the exact location of the positions.

4. The North point should be marked in the right-hand margin.

5. The following are a few important positions in the enemy lines, etc., which should be marked on the working map :—

(a) Loopholes, snipers' posts and observation posts.

(b) Machine-gun positions, known or suspected.

(c) Tracks to or from communication trenches, also tracks where the trench may be full of water or deep mud and the enemy gets out and walks a few yards on top. These are always good spots for the sniper to watch.

(d) Places where work is proceeding are always likely places for a good target. Also any other likely places for targets and best time to find them.

(e) R.E. dumps, stores, trench trams, etc. ; these can be marked on map from aeroplane photos.

(f) Suspected dummy trees, screens, dugouts, strong points, etc.

(g) Listening posts and paths or tracks to them.

(h) A range card should also accompany this map.

Conventional Signs.

Before preparing any military map it is most essential to have a knowledge of conventional signs. These signs should be uniform throughout an Army, otherwise information on a map might be most misleading as one unit's sign for an observation post might be another unit's sign for a machine-gun position, etc.

ROUTE REPORT.

Improved Method of describing a Route.

1. This method is similar to the civil motoring associations' " routes," with the difference that in this method the route runs **up** the page in the direction of the travel and is therefore easier to follow as it is " set " like a map.

2. In the absence of an adequate number of maps, this type of route could be easily cyclostyled and issued, or even dictated to a number of truck drivers, Section Commanders, etc., from one map.

3. This system is equally applicable to (*a*) a cross-country route for a patrol, or (*b*) a road journey for a truck driver.

4. The columns " Serial No. of Landmark " and " Milage," can be omitted or included as required.

A large arrow indicating direction of movement should always be shown, together with date, signature and heading.

Compass bearings may also assist in the case of 3 (*a*).

5. An example is shown opposite, suitable for a short road journey.

ROUTE No. 1.   *Classification A* 1.

Route : KING'S HEAD INN—CURZON BRIDGES via MYTCHETT LAKE.

Map Ref. : Aldershot Command.
Scale 1 inch.

Date of Recce. : 13 Apr. 39.

GENERAL REPORT.

1. This is an A1 road throughout. From a tactical point of view it is a dangerous one for movement as it contains many bridges over railways and canals. There is a bad bottleneck at 333745. Dangerous when in close proximity to the enemy.

2. All railway and canal bridges are constructed to carry any Army vehicle and contain ample clearance for same.

3. On the whole, the route gives good protection from the air except at TUNNEL HILL.

4. Owing to the number of turns on the road, the route should be picketed.

5. There are no milestones on the road.

6. FRIMLEY is a good billeting area.

7. Water can be obtained from MYTCHETT LAKE and the canal.

Route from : HOPE FARM (437610).
to : PADDLESWORTH (417316).
Ref. : Sheet 21B, 1 inch.

Serial Landmark	Route.	Milage.
7 ↑	PADDLESWORTH (417316)	3½
	800 yards	
	Good farm track	
6	Turn right through white gate	3
	¼ mile	
5	 PRESTON CH.	2¾
	¼ mile	
4	Under Railway Bridge ½ mile	
3	Turn left at NEW INN 1000 yards	2
2	Take right fork 600 yards on	
1		· 1
0	Approx. N.E. for 1 mile S.P. HOPE FM. (437610)	

(General direction N.E.)

J. JONES, *Lt.*,
1/Blank. Regt.

14 Jun. 39.

SECTION XVI

SNIPING IN ATTACK AND DEFENCE AND NIGHT SNIPING

There is still a great deal to be learnt about sniping in attack in trench warfare.

The tremendous artillery preparations and barrages have compelled us to modify some of our original instructions to snipers, because where front lines are at all close no sniper could possibly live in No Man's Land during a barrage.

During the Somme fighting snipers in several instances were able to put machine guns out of action by digging-in in front and waiting for them to open up.

The following notes give a rough outline of methods which should be employed by snipers in attack and defence in trench warfare.

Precautions.

Be most careful in the selection of your men. If this precaution is not taken it only means unnecessary casualties.

Men selected should not only be good scouts but good shots, and not only good shots but quick shots : men who can take rapid aim—what are sometimes called " off-hand " shots.

1. Sniping in Attack in Trench Warfare.

In an attack the bombardment usually comes first. Until this is over snipers should be kept more or less in reserve positions ; that is to say, if a big offensive is contemplated.

In the attack snipers should not be sent over with first rush of infantry. They should be on the lookout for enemy machine guns opening fire. These are difficult to distinguish from rifle fire ; use a telescope and observe greater escape of gas.

Snipers as a rule should operate on the flanks in an attack. If enemy has been roughly handled, snipers will watch for officers or N.C.Os. exposing themselves, directing operations, etc., re-forming men, and so on. Also shoot at men carrying loads of any sort.

If the advance is likely to be over 500 yards your best snipers might take up their positions just in front of enemy's front line in No Man's Land in shell holes. A Boche sniper did this on the Somme and laid out eight of our men before he was spotted.

If field of fire enables them to do so they should " dig in " on back edge of crater or shell hole, as shown in Fig. 1.

FIG. 1.

Some snipers have even taken a steel sniping plate out with them for protection against shrapnel, etc., during preliminary barrage, etc. They usually dig a narrow hole as per diagram and support the plate over their heads on two sticks.

FIG. 2.

Or on other occasions they also use this plate for sniping from craters as in Fig. 3.

Sitting Position.

FIG. 3.

The hole or hide must be as small as possible if for sniping. All excavated earth must be hidden. This is quite simple where the ground has been much cut up by shell fire.

Another method adopted by some snipers after shelling has diminished, is shown in Fig. 4.

1ˢᵗ Position   2ⁿᵈ Position.

FIG. 4.

When a trench is taken bring up snipers, but do not place them in the captured trench. They should work their way out in front, carefully watching for targets. Endeavour to obtain commanding position over some part of enemy's communication trenches or any of his trenches.

Keep in touch as much as possible, keep eyes open for useful information.

Observe as well as kill.

A good sniper-scout should be able to supply valuable information.

2. Attack by Night.

If we attack by night it is not advisable to use snipers unless they are also acting as scouts.

On a dark night snipers can be of no use. Only in case of counterattack by the enemy should snipers be called on, and in this case everyone must expect to turn out.

3. Open Warfare.

When enemy retires snipers should advance with the first wave and be given a roving commission.

Snipers should keep eyes open for enemy machine guns placed to retard our advance, and put these out of action if possible.

Snipers should act more or less as scouts in open warfare. It is impossible to lay down any particular rules to govern their actions. Experience, ingenuity, scoutcraft, marksmanship, keen observation, quick thought and action in awkward positions—any or all of these qualities may be called upon during an advance in open warfare.

They should have a good eye for ground, quickness in noting good positions other than on the ground, such as trees, houses, windmills, haystacks, etc. ; also knowledge and value of protective colour.

They must know of the danger of any careless movement when under observation, and have a good sense of direction (bump of location). They should continually look backward and note landmarks. This is most important.

4. Sniping in Defence.

The only means we have of annoying the enemy are :—

(1) Bombers.
(2) Snipers.
(3) Firing over Parapet.
(4) Machine Guns.

The chief object in defensive sniping is :—

(1) To kill.
(2) To observe.

To kill first of all the enemy sniper, hunt him out, spot his hides, lay for him. Draw his fire if you cannot spot him by any other means ; that is to say, make him shoot at dummy heads, etc.

Sniper and observer, if working together, should plan out their campaign for the day.

When the enemy attacks, snipers must not fire haphazard at anyone. Pick out officers, N.C.Os., machine-gunners, etc. Leave the mass to the mass.

Error of the Day.—When a sniper takes up his position, or before he takes up his position if possible, he should fire a shot to find error of day. This is better than a lot of theory. Fire at some range where you expect to get a target. Let the observer report carefully what happens. Choose a brick wall or clay bank or anything which would show strike of bullet. This shot should be fired very carefully because it will establish your elevation for the day most probably.

5. Sniping in Defence in Open Warfare.

Reverse the programme of attack in open warfare. Snipers must assist the rearguard to resist the enemy.

THE BATTALION INTELLIGENCE SECTION IN ATTACK IN TRENCH WARFARE, 1914-18 *

THE EMPLOYMENT OF OBSERVERS, SCOUTS AND SNIPERS BEFORE, DURING AND AFTER OPERATIONS.

Before the Attack.

Battalion Scouts.

1. The ground over which the battalion will advance must be carefully studied from observation posts and information forwarded to Brigade H.Q.

2. The information thus obtained should be annotated on aeroplane photo maps, either by Brigade H.Q. or the Battalion Intelligence Officer, and the maps issued to Company Commanders in order that they might be given a very good idea of the obstacles, if any, which would be encountered on the frontage allotted to them.

3. Failing an aeroplane photo map, all information must be plotted on skeleton maps of the battalion frontage and issued to all officers.

4. The Scout Officer and scouts will be detailed to make a thorough reconnaissance of the country behind our lines and report on trenches suitable for jumping-off trenches, also to reconnoitre an assembly area for the battalion.

5. Examine condition of our own wire and detail parties to cut passages for our troops during attack.

6. Scouts will also be used to guide companies to their positions in jumping-off trenches.

7. The Scout Officer with three or four scouts may be frequently detailed to lay a tape line for jumping-off positions for attacking companies.

8. Scouts should carefully patrol the whole front immediately before an attack and make sure there are no hidden obstacles, such as old trenches or ditches filled with barbed wire, no machine guns, etc. They should stay out watching carefully until the last minute, in case the enemy get wind of attack.

9. Also, when possible, to post scouts in advanced listening posts close to the enemy's defences, where sometimes, by lying quietly, it is possible to form an estimate of the garrison of the trench as well as to find out if any work is being done in the enemy trenches.

---

* It is hoped that, should the present war continue, the Battalion Intelligence Section will be granted an establishment and become recognized as the Battalion Intelligence Section on the same lines as in 1914-18.

10. Before an attack, No Man's Land must be frequently patrolled to prevent the enemy patrols from approaching our lines, also to observe enemy movements, wire work, etc.

11. By day, when not resting, scouts should look over the ground to be patrolled at night, memorize every detail of the ground, particularly if it is new to them, and make a sketch with landmarks, if any.

12. On the night before an attack all battalion scouts might be sent out to act as advanced listening posts to prevent hostile patrols from coming out.

13. If scouts move forward with the attack, they should take up their positions on the flanks.

14. Examine and report daily on condition of enemy wire.

15. Investigate reports that the enemy is withdrawing from his position.

16. Examine the effect of our artillery fire.

17. Prevent the enemy repairing his wire.

18. Scouts must be familiar with the location of all forward dumps.

19. Scouts act as guides to raiding parties.

20. When in reserve and moving up to the attack, usually in artillery formation, it is imperative to maintain proper interval and to keep in touch with formations in front, and in the rear with Battalion H.Q. ; for this purpose scouts can be used.

During and After the Attack.

Battalion Scouts.

1. Furnish escort for captured officers and N.C.Os. from Battalion H.Q. to Brigade H.Q.

2. Locate advanced Battalion H.Q. as H.Q. moves forward.

3. When battalion reaches its objective, scouts move to each flank and find out if the battalion is connected up and with whom.

4. Act as guides to special working parties or wiring parties.

5. Guide transport to new Battalion H.Q.

6. Act as guides to ammunition parties.

7. Confirm positions said to be taken up by companies and locate new Company H.Qs.

8. Take artillery and other officers to new positions.

9. Check up distances and positions.

10. Ascertain the numbers of all captured guns and their exact location.

11. Reconnoitre and report on the consolidation line as completed.

12. Scouts are used as leading file on offensive patrol in enemy communication trenches leading from captured positions for information.

13. When the objective is won, scouts and runners can to a certain extent be used in conjunction for purposes of communication. Contact must also be kept by scouts with battalions on flanks. Also contact and understanding between Intelligence and Scout Officers of flanking battalions. Patrolling must be carried out nightly on newly captured front.

14. During and after the attack, as the trenches become congested, scouts may be detailed to assist as far as possible in getting companies into position and directing other units.

Company Scouts.

1. Act as flank guides to their platoons in attack and maintain correct direction.

2. Carry out company patrols in conjunction with battalion scouts.

3. Guide parties of the company to various map locations.

4. Sometimes, owing to casualties, scouts may be used as company runners.

5. Supply guides to ration parties.

6. Used generally for Intelligence work with the company and to assist in reconnaissance, and in most cases should work under the direction of their Company Commanders.

Before, During and After Operations.

Battalion Observers.

1. The location of all observation posts, both infantry and artillery, should be reported as soon as they are established.

2. A diagram of the ground under observation should accompany the report whenever possible.

3. Night posts should be established to report on flare lights and enemy activity.

4. During all periods in the line, whenever possible two observation posts should be established per battalion.

5. Locate and man an S.O.S. post day and night.

6. Watch all movement behind enemy's lines.

7. Watch for any signs of the enemy massing or other movements of his troops and report to Artillery Liaison Officer.

8. Two battalion observers should be on duty night and day, one at or near Battalion H.Q. to warn H.Q. of any unusual occurrence, such as special flares, machine-gun fire, shelling, etc., and in the attack to watch for signal " Objective gained."

9. Trained observers should move forward close behind the attacking troops.

NOTE.—During the action of Vimy Ridge on the 9th April, 1917, an observation post was manned by two observers who were able to watch the advance of our troops and reported at 0535 (two minutes after the first wave jumped off) that the first trench had been taken. Half a minute later this information was transmitted to brigade.

This observation post reported as each trench was taken and also when the last wave of attack was clear of No Man's Land.

Company Observers.

1. During offensive operations Company Commanders should appoint previously trained observers.

2. Night and day one observer per company at least should be on duty.

3. Observations should be reported to the Company Commander at least twice a day.

4. If the frontage is an extended one, it is advisable for each platoon to have an observer and that reports be sent by Platoon Commander to Company Commander.

Snipers in Attack.

1. Snipers cannot be used effectively during the early stages of a big offensive in trench warfare, for what with bombs, barrages, rifle and machine-gun fire, the air is usually full of smoke and visibility consequently bad. On this account telescopic sights would be useless and open sights nearly so.

2. Also during the early stages of an attack, when the creeping barrage is on, very few enemy snipers will be bold enough to expose themselves, and it has been found that the attacking troops are well able to deal with the escaping enemy.

3. It was found in the war of 1914-18 that German snipers took a very heavy toll during the consolidation of our lines, and far better results were obtained by holding back the best shots until the final objective was gained and consolidation began.

4. The snipers should be given a roving commission, and Platoon Commanders and Company Commanders should take the earliest opportunity of advising sniping and Intelligence Officers of any casualties occurring by enemy sniping, and the location of the casualty.

Battalion in Attack.

1. The services of the Intelligence Section can be invaluable in gathering and forwarding information to Battalion H.Q.

2. It should be the duty of the Intelligence Officer to collect and communicate all messages received from his section to his Battalion Commander and, in addition, to transmit the information to flanking units and Brigade according to the urgency and means available.

3. Stations should not be closed until more advanced ones are established. If the O.C. moves forward, an officer should remain behind to receive messages for him.

4. The Battalion Intelligence Officer, with the Battalion Scout Officer and battalion scouts, should accompany the Battalion Commander and remain at Battalion H.Q. until the attack is well under way, when the Scout Officer with selected scouts should follow the attack, pressing on behind the leading waves, with the object of locating advanced report centre and ultimately Battalion H.Q. ; also to send back reports of the situation and possibly, in conjunction with company scouts, push out patrols in front, and generally keep in touch and report on situations.

5. Observers will be watching the progress of the advance and, on further objectives being gained, will establish forward observation posts.

6. When the final objective is gained the Battalion Intelligence Officer and four scouts should advance and make a thorough reconnaissance of the new positions, establish contact with the units on the flanks and find out who they are, and prepare a fairly accurate map showing location of units.

7. Battalion snipers will remain at Battalion H.Q. until final objectives are gained, when they will be sent forward to cover consolidation and harass the enemy as much as possible.

8. Observers should be constantly employed and Intelligence Reports sent in to brigade twice daily during the advance and from all newly established positions.

Taking Over during Operations.

When taking over a frontage during operations and prior possibly to a further contemplated advance, the Scout Officer and six scouts should make a complete reconnaissance of the forward area, and should visit all outposts and post observers and snipers. Whenever possible it is advisable for the Adjutant to accompany the Scout Officer when making this reconnaissance of the front line in order to locate the disposition of companies and outposts and location of report centre.

NOTE.—After the Battle of Vimy Ridge, Battalion Commanders were requested to forward a report to Corps H.Q., stating how their Battalion Intelligence Sections were employed during the action, together with suggestions for future operations.

The following are a few extracts from these reports :—

Scouts.

" The Intelligence Officer, five snipers, three observers and four scouts went behind the second wave and established battalion forward observation post, report centre and temporary forward Battalion H.Q. Fired green signal to advise observation post in rear that forward report centre was established, and scout sent back to Battalion H.Q. to bring up O.C. and H.Q. staff."

" The battalion scouts were not sent over in the actual attack, but were retained for purposes of reconnaissance afterwards."

" Battalion scouts were not sent over with the waves of the attack, but were kept at Battalion H.Q. for the purpose of obtaining information after the attack. As soon as the attack had developed the scouts were sent out in pairs at stated intervals with instructions to establish S.O.S. posts, forward observation posts, and generally to report on situation."

" All scouts were returned to their companies for the attack and one scout in each company was told to check up the situation on reaching objective and then report to Battalion H.Q. Only one scout reported back ; remainder were either killed or wounded."

" The method of sending battalion scouts over the top with their companies I consider to be a mistake because they may all become casualties. It would be better to retain them until some time later and then utilize them for purposes of reconnaissance by their respective companies."

Snipers.

" Not only were our snipers active and most helpful in keeping down enemy sniping (which at that time was very bad), but the scouts also obtained valuable information."

" After final objective had been carried and during consolidation, daylight hours were utilized by the snipers in forward isolated positions with splendid results."

" Owing to the rapidity of advance and heavy artillery fire, snipers had very little chance of engaging targets during first phase of the attack, but did good work in keeping down the fire of enemy snipers while battalion was digging in."

Battalion Intelligence Section in Attack.

A Brigade Commander states that—

" In future operations it has been decided to hold back Intelligence Sections until the objective is gained and then employ them in observation, scouting and sniping."

PATROLLING

GENERAL.

Importance and Uses of.

1. Keep upper hand in No Man's Land.

2. To amplify observation.

3. Learn exact nature of ground.

4. To see and feel what cannot be seen in the ordinary way (dead ground).

5. To prove observation.

6. To confirm ideas as to suspicious objects.

7. To look for enemy movements, particularly in No Man's Land.

8. To give timely warning of or to stop enemy action.

9. To secure own troops against surprise.

10. Protection.

11. To keep in touch with enemy after successful attack.

12. Communication with flanks.

13. To reconnoitre line of advance.

There are three important types of patrol, the two main ones being Reconnaissance and Fighting :—

                (1) Reconnaissance.

                (2) Fighting.

                (3) Standing.

Also, in trench warfare, listening post.

Brief Description of each.

1. Reconnaissance.—Four men maximum ; information without fighting, but always prepared to fight. As lightly equipped and as small in numbers as possible.

2. Fighting.—Must be a self-contained unit ; seldom less than one platoon ; multiples of four ; fully armed but lightly equipped ; Bren or " gangster " guns, bombs. Must be tough in spirit and deed ; information, and prepared to fight for it.

3. Standing.—As an ambush or to guard approaches ; may move or withdraw ; section or more, with light machine gun. (cf. Sentry group—last man, last round.)

4. Listening Post.—Two men ; information by eye and ear.

Formations used are shown in the following diagrams :—

FORMATION OF RECONNAISSANCE PATROL.

NOTE. —Distances and intervals : By day, seeing distance (10 to 15 yds.).
By night, almost touching. When halted, to be able to face outwards
and touch heel to heel.

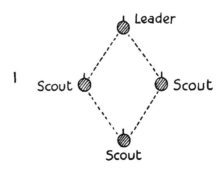

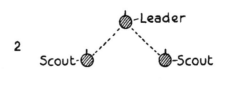

NOTE.—" Gangster " guns: Four or five per battalion, probably Thompson on sling.

N.B.—The Thompson gun is the patrol leader's gun and should be carried by him or someone right next door to him, more or less as his " loader."

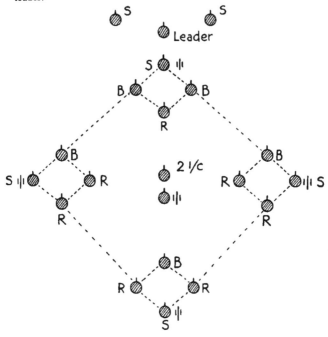

il - Thompson Gangster Gun

S - Scouts

R - Riflemen

B - Bomber   21 men
                             all told'

RECONNAISSANCE PATROL.

In Open Warfare.

Objects.
1. Information *re* enemy.
2. Protection.
3. To guard against surprise.
4. To prevent enemy encroachment by night.
5. To reconnoitre line of advance.
6. To keep touch with enemy after successful attack.
7. To obtain particulars of enemy defences.

Preparations before starting out.
1. Leader studies map and ground and makes plan.
2. Looks for covered routes.
3. Looks for bounds.
4. Looks for places where might be ambush.
5. Everyone must know orders.

Information given to all before Patrol goes out.
To anyone in forward defended localities, or who is likely to be there when patrol goes out.

1. Time of starting.

2. Approximate time of return.

3. Place of starting ; approximate route and intended place of return.

4. Strength. Any prearranged signals.

ORDERS FOR RECONNAISSANCE PATROL.

1. Information.
   - (a) Enemy.
   - (b) Own troops. Forward defended localities.
2. Intention. Definitely and clearly expressed ; a definite task.
3. Method.
   - (a) Strength.
   - (b) Formations in detail—
     - Concealment.
     - Control.
     - Protection.
     - Ground.
   - (c) Commander.
   - (d) Second in command.
   - (e) Leaves at ....
   - (f) Returns .... approximately.
   - (g) Route.
   - (h) Action if attacked.

4. Administration.

   (a) Equipment. (In open warfare when covering more ground probably more worn than in trench warfare.)

   (b) Bombs, etc. Wire-cutters.

   (c) Badges and papers (left behind).

   (d) Feeding (before going out and hot drink on return).

5. Communication.

   (a) Password.

   (b) Flank units.

   (c) Signs and signals prearranged.

   (d) Platoon and company headquarters.

   (e) ANY QUESTIONS.

NOTE.—In issuing orders to patrols the following facilities must be given : They must have all known information, including aeroplane photographs and maps. They must have an opportunity of studying by day the ground to be covered at night.

General.

1. Move in bounds.

2. Frequent halts.

3. Route. Look for covered approach and places to observe from. Do not use same way twice running.

4. Approach. Never do what enemy expects—*i.e.*, go round flanks or rear rather than frontally.

5. Avoid obvious isolated cover.

6. Avoid enemy patrols. Job to get information without fighting.

7. No coughs or colds.

8. Dogs. Kicked by all except by master.

In Trench Warfare.

Objects.

1. Information *re* enemy trenches and wire.
2. Identification.
3. Special tasks.
4. Control No Man's Land.

Preparations before Starting Out.

As for open warfare, but using periscopes to study ground.

Information before Patrol Goes Out.

To anyone on duty or who is likely to be on duty on the battalion front in the front line during the time the patrol is out.

As for open war, but add flank units must be informed.

Senior member of patrol must inform senior person in line when his patrol has returned, intact or not.

Orders.

Same sequence as for open warfare.

General.

Reconnaissance Patrol should be as small as possible. They should avoid contact ; must be prepared to fight. Various formations such as file, arrow-head, etc., are used for patrols, but the formation demonstrated by the Canadians to the Guards Division in 1918 is probably the best. They made it a rule that every patrol should be multiples of four. Four, therefore, is probably the best number for a Reconnaissance Patrol, although very tricky tasks are often better performed by one or two men. The patrol proceeds as follows :—

The leader, officer or N.C.O., looks to his front and is responsible for direction. The second man watches the right flank, the third man the left, and the fourth man the rear. When the patrol halts, as it must frequently, the four men lie down in diamond formation immediately with their feet touching. Thus every flank is watched and each man can signal his neighbour by touching his feet. If the patrol is crawling all they have to do is for numbers two, three and four to crawl until they are all facing outwards. A Reconnaissance Patrol obviously must travel as light as possible. Revolvers, clubs, two bombs a head. Better without gas masks, which invariably show and make a rustling noise when crawling. Equipment definitely left behind.

Special Points.

1. Not more than one patrol out at a time.

2. Greatest care in marking gap for return through wire.

3. Greatest care in leaving trench ; desultory fire continues.

4. A dark, dirty, rainy night is the best time for patrolling.

5. When Very lights and star shells catch the patrol they must remain motionless whatever position they are in. This is also very helpful for patrol to observe.

6. Patience is the secret of successful patrolling.

7. They must frequently stop in diamond formation and listen. They must crawl feet and inches at a time if necessary. All communication must be by sign and not a word must be spoken.

8. One officer only ; two leads to arguments.

9. Patrols frequently left out too long in No Man's Land. Two hours are sufficient owing to the strain.

10. Company Commanders must never send officers or N.C.Os. in charge of patrols if they suffer from night blindness or defective hearing.

11. Luminous watches should not be worn on the wrist, except turned round on the inside of the wrist.

12. Keep in hollows.

FIGHTING PATROL.

In Open Warfare.

Objects.
1. Some special purpose.
2. Delay enemy during own withdrawal.
3. Counter enemy patrolling.
4. Cover own troops forming up for attack.
5. Identifications and prisoners.
6. Harass enemy.
7. Cover demolition party.

Preparations before Starting Out.
As for Reconnaissance Patrol.

Information given to all before Patrol goes out.
As for Reconnaissance Patrol.

Orders.
As for Reconnaissance patrol, but with following exceptions :—
Strength, one platoon or more.
Formation.
Equipment : Lightly equipped and fully armed ; bayonets fixed.

General.
1. Must be tough.
2. Act offensively.
3. Strong enough to deal with enemy patrols.
4. Bring back own wounded.

In Trench Warfare.

Objects.
1. To collect a prisoner for identification.
2. To engage other enemy patrols.
3. To break up enemy working parties.
4. Generally to maintain command in No Man's Land.

Preparations before Starting Out.
As for Reconnaissance Patrol.

Information before Patrol Goes Out.
As for Reconnaissance Patrol, but warn sentries and observation posts, also.

Orders.
Same sequence as for Reconnaissance Patrol.

155

General.

1. Go out prepared to fight.

2. No hard-and-fast rule as to exact strength. Generally one platoon at least.

3. No hard-and-fast rule as to formations, but following rules must be observed :—

    (a) Formation must be a suitable one, capable of being maintained under worst conditions.

    (b) The Bren or " gangster " gun must be well protected, but able to fire at a moment's notice.

    (c) The officer must lead the patrol. Second-in-command in the centre or rear.

    (d) Formation shown was particularly mobile in all kinds of light and weather.

    (e) The Bren can come into action in any direction in a few seconds and has adequate protection.

    (f) Each section forms a fighting unit in the event of being cut off temporarily.

    (g) Front, flanks and rear protected by trained scouts.

4. Equipment. The following will be carried : Rifles, bayonet fixed ; bandolier of S.A.A. ; bomb in pocket ; wire-cutters ; cap comforters.

Preparation.

Enemy posts frequently form good objects for identification, but in order to bring off a successful result with the minimum casualties a good deal of care is necessary.

Information.

Before starting the most important things to know are :—

    (a) Location of post.

    (b) Strength of post.

    (c) Wire.

    (d) Blocks.

    (e) Light machine gun or trench mortar covering post.

    (f) Direction from which reinforcements are likely to come.

Attack—Points to Remember.

1. Practically never try to rush a post with a frontal attack.

2. Two parties are generally more successful than one : one on each flank or one to come up from the rear.

3. If one flank of the post should be protected it is generally best to use one party to engage the enemy from the front, while the other party works round to the flank and makes the actual attack.

4. It is always as well to remind the attacking party that light machine guns and trench mortars covering the posts are to place their barrage line well in front of the post, and there is, therefore, very little danger from them once the attacking party is close to the post, except in the retirement.

NOTE.—Fighting patrols are not always covered in this way.

5. Once in the post, a few smoke bombs thrown in the trench and behind the post as a screen will render valuable assistance to the success of the raid. Very few men will attempt to come through the smoke barrage to see what is going on on the other side. It is also of great value in covering the retirement.

6. The retirement should always be carried out with the same amount of care as the actual attack. More casualties have been due to a poor retirement than in the attack itself.

7. No firing without orders from patrol leader.

Precautions.

Make sure that any relieving sentries are warned if relief should take place while the patrol is still out in No Man's Land. The greatest care must be taken if it becomes necessary to alter any messages which have already been communicated to any sentries, etc.

	S	Scouts ...	...	...	...	...	3
	R	Riflemen	...	...	...	...	4
	B	Bombers	...	...	...	...	6
	L	Leader ...	...	...	...	...	· 1
2nd i/c		Second-in-Command ...		...		...	1
L.M.G.		(or " gangster " gun if available)				...	2
							17

INTELLIGENCE

A GENERAL SUMMARY

Popular Fallacies.

At the commencement of the last war, and for a considerable time subsequently, Intelligence was looked upon as a species of black art by the majority of our troops of all ranks. It was thought by many to be much too profound a subject for fighting troops, and certain Intelligence Officers were credited with almost superhuman divination and spoken of with bated breath.

To-day we know that we fight on Intelligence. We know that Intelligence and Action must go hand in hand together. If no system is adopted whereby they can be co-ordinated, then any intelligence acquired will be of small value.

Action is the Word.

A system of trench warfare makes it very difficult for the Intelligence organization to know very far ahead when and where the enemy will attack. He can move large masses of troops by night in a most rapid manner and reinforce any particular frontage without exciting suspicion.

Bombardments, instead of lasting for days, will be reduced to a few hours or even minutes, so that we cannot rely on them to give us sufficient time to prepare. This helps to emphasize the importance of Action on receipt of Intelligence.

In any future war, Time when applied to Intelligence will be vital. In order that Action may be taken immediately on receipt of Intelligence, it is important—

(a) To obtain uniformity of method in General Staff (Intelligence) work throughout a Corps.

(b) At the same time to ensure that the best use is being made of information. In order to obtain this uniformity of method it will be necessary to have a system thoroughly organized.

Organization.

CORPS H.Q.

G.S.O.2 (Intelligence) with six or seven Officer Assistants ; Intelligence Corps Officers, for handling of prisoners, documents, knowledge of German language and organization.

Flash spotting.

Survey Section, Topographical Section, Maps.

Corps Observers, etc. etc.

DIVISION.
  G.S.O.2 (Intelligence).
  Two or three Assistant Officers.
BRIGADE.
  Staff Captain (Intelligence).
BATTALION.
  Battalion Intelligence Officer.

General Staff Officer.

In order that Intelligence may be carried out satisfactorily, the General Staff Officer—

(a) Must have a thorough knowledge of both our own and enemy tactics.

(b) Must be thoroughly acquainted with the nature, method of employment and potentialities of all supporting arms.

(c) Must be sufficiently senior and sufficiently experienced to ensure that commanders of various units will place reliance on his deductions and suggestions.

He is responsible for—

(a) Liaison between the infantry and supporting arms down to battalion sectors.

(b) Collecting and distributing all information regarding the enemy's dispositions and defences opposite his division.

(c) Co-ordinating the fields of view of infantry observation posts and communications to and from them in divisional area.

(d) During active operations, working out the probable assembly positions, lines of approach or lines of counter-attack which might be used by the enemy.

(e) Co-ordinating the requests of attacking infantry brigades for destructive shoots—Air services—Harassing fire on the divisional front as a whole.

(f) Ensuring that the best possible use is made of the Signal service.

(g) Preparing maps and reports concerning our own defences.

Divisional Artillery Intelligence.

Artillery Brigade Intelligence is detailed in conjunction with Battalion Intelligence.

Reconnaissance Officer.

(a) Maintains close touch with G.S.O.2 (I.) of infantry division and works with him in developing Intelligence organization.

(b) Collects all Intelligence obtained from artillery observation posts and issues same in the form of a Daily Intelligence Summary.

(c) Is generally responsible for Office Records in so far as they pertain to information regarding enemy territory.

To Sum Up—

It may be said that General Intelligence is the basis of all military operations. By General Intelligence is meant the following :—

- (a) How the enemy holds his trenches.
- (b) Where his dugouts are.
- (c) Where his supports for counter-attack are billeted.
- (d) Where his Battalion H.Q. is.
- (e) Where his Company H.Q. is.
- (f) How his troops come up to the line.
- (g) Where his machine guns are.
- (h) Where his trench mortars are.
- (i) Where his guns are.
- (j) Divisional, Regimental, Battalion, Company } boundaries.
- (k) Average strength of his companies.

To deal with above information an efficient organization is required.

Deductions from Information.

In forwarding information from the front line careful deductions must be made from facts, not facts postulated from deductions. One must not jump to conclusions. Always state how information was acquired ; try to confirm it from every available source. Old information is of no value. Accuracy of detail is most important.

Sources of Information.

The chain of responsibility is roughly as follows :—

War Office Intelligence.—Thoroughly acquainted with German organization in Berlin area.

G.H.Q.—In possession of important information nearer the front.

Army.—Nearer still.

Corps.—The tactical unit where man watches man.

The nearer the front the more reliable is the information.

Aeroplanes.—In ordinary times not of much value for reporting isolated movement, particularly of individuals.

As a general rule very little movement seen behind German lines, whereas they reported immense amount of movement by comparison behind our lines.

During an attack the aeroplane is of great value when co-operating with infantry and tanks and locating units and reporting hostile troops. This information is usually accurate. So much takes place during the night that one cannot rely on aeroplanes as a security for information of immediately impending attack.

Aeroplane Photos.—Remarkable strides have been made by us in aero-photography from the point of view of Intelligence. For a long time the interpretation of aeroplane photos was considered feasible only by a few men in the armies whose services were therefore considered almost priceless. During the latter part of the last war this was proved quite a fallacy.

An aeroplane photo is a thing which any man of average intelligence and experience can understand after a week's instruction. But in position warfare the expert camouflage artist can deceive the most expert interpreter of photos ; this has been proved.

The great function of photos is to use them as corroborative evidence in conjunction with reports. Also to check statements of prisoners. It is also important to compare old photos of certain positions with new ones of the same locality ; therefore the former should not be destroyed.

Indications of attack are now extraordinarily small and hardly noticeable unless one is on the look-out.

The following are a few instances of indications of attack foretold by photos :—

BEFORE ARRAS-SCARPE ATTACK, APRIL, 1918.

The north flank of the attack was heavily wired.

Improving roads ; if cut up by our shell fire, they were rebuilt.

New roads on flanking army fronts.

Three days before attack large increase in size of ammunition dumps ; this was corroborated by a prisoner.

BEFORE ATTACK ON THIRD ARMY FRONT, 1918.

Scallop-shaped workings were spotted from photos ; these were in the wire in front of support trenches and connected by a trail or new road to main road. These proved to be positions prepared for forward guns in case of successful advance.

LA BASSÉE FRONT.

In order to get our " wind up " on a front where the enemy had no immediate intention of attacking, he assembled numerous dummy tanks and obvious dummy camouflage on poles to represent new gun positions.

BEFORE ATTACK ON FIRST ARMY FRONT, APRIL 9TH, 1918.

Two days before this attack aeroplane photos revealed valuable information—
>   All villages in back areas were full of traffic.
>   Gardens were full of troops and vehicles.
>   Village squares were full of traffic.

This was a particularly unusual occurrence for the Boche in daytime. But the most important information, and that which clinched matters regarding the imminence of attack, was the fact that large numbers of foot bridges had been placed close to water courses in readiness for the attack.

Deductions from photos were perfectly accurate in these cases.

Battalion Intelligence Officer.

It is pointed out in another Section how important it is for this officer to study photos in conjunction with reports of his observers and scouts and his log map.

Prisoners and Identifications.

A prisoner is, of course, himself an identification. During offensive operations or a battle it will be possible each night to know through prisoners how many divisions have been against us.

Prisoners must be examined and their unit reported.

Then comes the question of obtaining detailed information from prisoners. Men selected for this purpose should be the only people allowed to examine prisoners. An amateur might very quickly put a prisoner on his guard and cause him to retain valuable information. Suggestion, and knowledge of German organization, is the main thing in handling prisoners.

It is important to induce prisoners to confirm information suggested to them.

Handling of Prisoners.

Officers of the Intelligence Corps all have their own particular methods of conducting an interrogation in order to obtain the best results.

In some cases prisoners are made to stand severely to attention and are interrogated roughly, but it is the general consensus of opinion that it is productive of much more satisfactory results to interrogate prisoners in a friendly way. Let them sit down in a chair and in some cases let them smoke. Reference is here made to particular prisoners, when important information is urgently required.

Documents.

Second in value only to prisoners.

Documents are most important and must be sent on with prisoner and **not** retained until next day. The Boche usually keeps his papers in his tail pocket, whereas the Britisher carries his over his heart. Letters and postcards, particularly the latter, have produced valuable information ; this is not generally realized.

It was always the custom of the German soldier to write his name and unit on his postcard ; each postcard had the postmark of the Field Post Station, which were all numbered, the location of each one being very soon known to us. As postcards were usually dated, it was possible to know where a certain unit was on a certain date.

Some extraordinarily valuable information was written by the Boche on postcards. Movements of troops in particular—economic conditions also.

During the progress of a continuous battle, as for instance from March to November, 1918, thousands and thousands of postcards and documents were collected on the battlefield, not only from prisoners and the dead, but scattered all over the ground.

Balloons.

Not of much value from the point of view of infantry Intelligence. They have an oblique line of sight and are much hampered by mist and fog. Have been termed the Divisional Commander's observation post. Useful for spotting gun flashes and general situation as regards shelling.

Movements of units smaller than a complete company of infantry or battery will probably escape notice.

Useful as a Signal Report Station for receiving messages from forward units on the ground.

Pigeons.

As a means for obtaining information from enemy country their use was discontinued during the later stages of the war ; but used within our own lines.

Sound Ranging.

    (a) Can locate hostile batteries firing.
    (b) Can locate hostile shell burst.
    (c) Can determine calibre of gun.
    (d) Can detect dummy flashes.
    (e) Can only work efficiently when both strength and direction of the wind are favourable.
    (f) Cannot obtain results when very heavy firing is going on.
    (g) Can be put out of action by having lines cut by hostile shell fire.
    (h) Is hampered by lack of mobility.

Microphone.—The microphone is the principal instrument used.

Sound is photographed and measured and by mathematical calculation bearing and intersection can be obtained.

Undershock.—Mistakes frequently occur when men are new at the game of sound ranging through the error of giving a bearing on the undershock sound.

When a gun fires there are two sounds : one caused by the shell when its velocity is greater than sound—namely, when for a short distance it is travelling faster than sound—and the other a fainter noise coming more slowly from the gun.

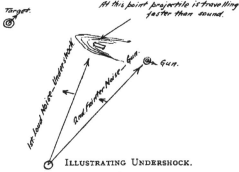

ILLUSTRATING UNDERSHOCK.

Flash Spotters.

These are divided into groups and arranged in a very similar manner to the sound-ranging system. Each group has a number of observation posts connected to a central headquarters. By means of a special apparatus observation of two or more posts on a hostile gun flash can be synchronized and the position of gun determined by means of intersection, tri-section, etc.

Flash spotters usually operate with the heavy artillery and belong to the Army.

Wireless (E).

By means of special instruments, hostile observing planes and sending stations can be approximately located and their wireless calls intercepted. They can give early warning of a hostile plane about to range.

This system is useful in view of any change in the distribution of hostile observing planes and sending stations, which can be at once noted and inferences drawn.

Intelligence Branch or I.B.

The existence of this branch of the Intelligence system only became better known towards the end of the last war. Its particular functions are to prevent the collection, recording or communicating of information likely to be useful either directly or indirectly to the enemy, such as propaganda, rumours, cable cutting, destruction of bridges and factories, etc.

Organization.—Called the Intelligence Police.

> 60-100 in each army (6-8 officers).
> Four sub-areas in an army.
> 12-15 Intelligence Police in each sub-area.
> 1 Officer set aside for railway control.

All cases of a suspicious nature should be referred at once to the nearest I.B. H.Q.

Prevention of Espionage.—Dropping or landing agents by parachute from aeroplanes.

Use of disguises.
Visits to friends.
Prostitutes.
Tea-rooms.

Also during active operations and in view of an advance, spies would be left behind our lines with the population. Women have been found to be particularly dangerous in the matter of stealing documents.

Spies disguised as our own troops.

Very few agents were caught in the British zone owing to the close surveillance maintained.

Schemes.—Embroidered postcards with name of regiment.

Officers' cheques : Agents cashing them to obtain name and location of regiment.

Advertisements in Paris papers. Women inviting officers to correspond with them, thereby getting name and location of unit.

Telephones in cellars.
Windmills.
Clocks, hands of.
Smuggled letters.
Wireless.
Floating messages down a river.
Laying cable under sea close along seashore between Dunkirk and Ostend.

Restrictions.—There were severe restrictions on the civil population both as regards residents and transients.

All had identity cards with photo and full particulars. Those not of French nationality were obliged to have special paper.

Railway Control.—Most important. Spies nearly always travelled by train. Civilian passengers checked either on the train or passed through an office.

Civilian motor cars vigorously inspected (Blue Permits).

Repatries carefully watched.

I.B. officer became intimate with civil population of his area. These officers were not or should not be frequently changed and very soon spot any stranger arriving in an area. These officers received great help from the civilians.

Intelligence T. or I.T.

This refers to listening sets for intercepting hostile messages and disclosing indiscreet telephone conversations carried out by ourselves when in close proximity to the front line.

Information on the following points must neither be given nor asked by telephone or buzzer near front-line trenches except by code :—

- (a) Names of commanders, officers, H.Q., units, places ; positions ; map references (references to observation posts, etc.) ; machine-gun positions and H.Q. ; dumps ; railways ; trench mortar emplacements.

- (b) Movement of troops, such as patrols, reliefs, working parties, transport, batteries, aeroplanes, arrival of reinforcements.

- (c) R.E. indents, ammunition returns, casualty returns, burial returns, situation reports, strength of units.

- (d) Position of our troops, rest billets, training schools.

- (e) Impending operations such as raids, artillery or trench mortar bombardments, aeroplanes, mines, gas.

- (f) The effect of any of the enemy's operations against us.

- (g) Observation of the enemy's movements, any reference to prisoners or deserters, or any statements made by them.

All unnecessary gossip by telephone or " buzzer " must be stopped.

Misuse by our Troops.—Apart from valuable information obtained about the enemy, our listening sets intercepted many messages and a good deal of telephonic conversation on our own lines close to the front containing much military information which would have been of considerable value to the enemy.

A few instances from First Army front :—

(a) " Tell the officer only one patrol is going out to-night."

(b) A message mentioning the 24th Division.

(c) " I had to meet a party of Canadians " (23rd October, 1916).

(d) Reference to 5th Canadian Infantry Brigade Pioneers (22nd October, 1916).

> NOTE.—The last two messages gave away the arrival of the Canadian Corps on the First Army front.

(e) " 10th Royal Fusiliers. Please be at C.O.'s office at 10 a.m."

(f) " The O.C. London Scottish has just been in to see me and is on his way down to you. He wants us to take over that bit of line on our left that got smashed in. Do not do anything until you get orders."

(g) Also various messages regarding reliefs giving positions of trench mortars, machine guns, etc.

A few more examples from fronts of other armies, all of which the Boche intercepted :—

(a) " Why did witness not attend at Boeschape on 7th. Division demand report."

(b) " What battalion is in the line now ?"   " The 10th Inniskillings."

(c) " You have challenged South Wales Borderers to a football match to-morrow, haven't you ?"

Most of the German messages were sent in cipher and some were deciphered. Codes are used for all messages of any importance. The Germans as a rule preserved much stricter discipline with regard to telephone conversations than was the case with our own troops.

History of Listening Sets.

They were used by the French and Germans after April, 1915 ; by ourselves after about April, 1916. Many experiments were tried by all three armies before satisfactory results were obtained.

Fullerphones cannot be overheard by the enemy. Where installed they may be used for sending by key any message in clear. They are no protection in the case of spoken messages.

Anti-Aircraft.

Can and do procure most valuable information. The German was found to be very methodical in conducting his movements in the air. Previous to an attack he always reconnoitred the country over which he intended to advance by means of aerial observation.

The German's big attack on March 21st, 1918, was expected by A.A., and the actual flanks and depth of the Boche advance were charted.

Anti-aircraft organization with regard to the siting of their observation posts was somewhat similar to the sound rangers and flash spotters.

These covered a certain area under an officer who directed them from a central station.

ANTI·AIRCRAFT DIAGRAM

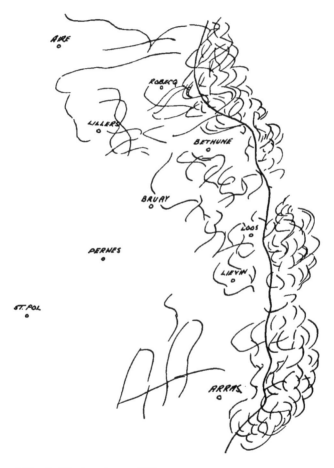

AIRE

ROBECQ

LILLERS

BETHUNE

BRUAY

LOOS

PERNES

LIEVIN

ST. POL

ARRAS

MAY 31ST TO JUNE 6TH 1918.

Each observation post had a map, and on this map was marked or plotted by special device the flight of each Boche plane over our lines. So that after a certain time, if he had been very active, certain portions of the front were covered with masses of thin black lines.

Intelligence which directs the Fire of Guns.

In this case we have to deal with the enormous cost of munitions as used by the artillery and with what ease the efforts of our munition workers can be wasted by inaccurate fire direction.

Those primarily responsible for directing fire are : Ground observers, balloon observers, aeroplanes.

Accurate intelligence is very essential when it becomes necessary to direct the fire of large-calibre guns, such as the 14-in. high-velocity on railway mounting.

The cost of this gun in 1914-18 was ...	£250,000
Weight	250 tons.
Length	52 ft.
Shell weighed	1,560 lb.
Cost	£1,800
Range	34,000 yards.

Not only is it necessary to direct accurately the fire of these heavy guns, but all guns and everything else, particularly fire which will minimize our own casualties.

Intelligence in Battle.

Principal sources from which Intelligence is received in open warfare :—

1. Reports from fighting units.

2. R.A.F. contact patrols and aeroplane reconnaissance.

3. Balloon observers.

4. Prisoners and captured documents.

5. Field Survey Company observation groups.

6. Artillery Forward Observation Officers.

7. Corps observation groups.

8. Anti-aircraft sections.

9. Information received from higher sources—Secret Services.

10. Reports from other armies and other formations.

AEROPLANE PHOTOGRAPHS

TYPES OF PHOTOGRAPHS.

Aeroplane photographs can be divided into three main types, vertical, oblique and stereoscopic.

1. Vertical photographs are taken for different purposes at varying heights, and are the general photograph in use.

" Mosaics "—*i.e.*, photographs assembled to form a complete photographic map of a given area—are useful for giving a comprehensive view of lines of defence, which can be readily compared with isolated photographs taken later.

2. Oblique photographs may be considered as a panoramic view of the area covered by the vertical photograph, and the two, when possible, should be examined together. They contain much valuable topographical detail and indicate the general slopes and contours.

3. Stereoscopic photographs have now come into general use and are of the greatest value in determining detail not easily seen on the ordinary vertical photograph, such as the comparative relief of different objects. They should be employed whenever possible.

Stereoscopic oblique photographs, which show undulations of ground, however small, are very valuable in the study of ground prior to an offensive, and should be used in conjunction with the map, to indicate features of tactical importance which may not be shown on the map.

Method of setting up Stereoscopic Photographs.

To obtain a stereoscopic effect, take two photographs of the same object (two copies of the same photograph will not do, a fact which is not always recognized) and place one photograph on the top of the other, so that the features on one coincide with the same features on the other.

Draw the top photograph aside, keeping the features under examination parallel the whole time, until, at about two inches apart, the images will again fit, and houses and trees will stand up as in nature.

The photographs must be placed in the order in which they were taken—*i.e.*, the left-hand picture on the left side—as otherwise the features will appear reversed, and houses will sink into holes and cuttings will become embankments.

At first, the number of images may be confusing, but a few minutes' practice will be enough to accustom the eyes to pick up the two required.

GENERAL.

The Examination of Photographs.

Before examining a photograph it is necessary to form an idea of the appearance of objects from above, and to try to realize that objects will not appear under their usual aspect as seen from the ground. This is due to the fact that only the tops of the objects appear on the photograph.

During the actual examination of a photograph, the following important points should be remembered :—

1. The best available map should be studied with great care, so that the configuration of the ground and the salient features are familiar. On no account should a photograph be studied without a map. To locate the exact position of the photograph, it is necessary to set the photograph with the map, by the aid of the north point which is marked on each photograph.

2. An approximate idea of the scale of the photograph should be formed by comparing the distance between two fixed points on the photograph with the same points on the map.

3. Having ascertained the position of the photograph on the map, and the scale, it is now necessary before examining the detail of the photograph to ascertain the direction of the light. This can be done by studying the direction in which shadows are thrown by trees, houses, shell holes, etc. The photograph should then be held so that the shadows fall towards one.

Shadows are the most important factor in the study of photographs. Only by a careful examination of their shape is it possible to ascertain the size or shape of the objects which cast them.

In the same way it is possible to determine whether an object is concave or convex.

A thorough familiarity with the effect of cast shadows is an absolute essential to the correct study and easy interpretation of air photographs.

4. Photographs should be examined systematically by the aid of a pointer, and beginners should be warned against looking at a photograph as a whole rather than concentrating their attention on each detail.

5. In examining a photograph, it is necessary to keep in one's mind each possible interpretation of any particular detail ; the various probabilities must be taken into account. It must then be determined whether there is sufficient evidence to justify a definite decision.

General Conclusions.

The general policy of the enemy, whether offensive or defensive, is indicated by a study of air photographs, read in conjunction with information from other sources.

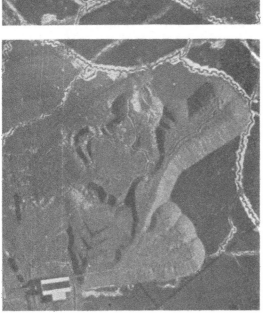

Light and Shadow.

Photographs illustrating the effect of viewing a slag heap, one with the light and the other against the light. The correct way is to study a photograph looking against the direction of light, which is photograph No. 2. With photograph No. 1 an excavation is apparently seen, and in No. 2 a raised object.

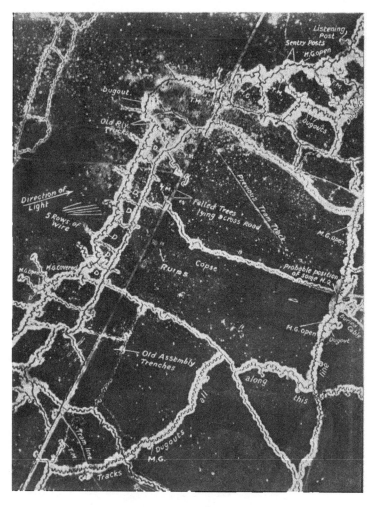

Annotated Trench Photograph.

Offensive Preparations.

1. A sudden increase in the artillery activity, in the number of battery positions and in new aerodromes.

2. An increase in the number of communication trenches.

3. An increase in the light railways and dumps.

4. A series of saps pushed forward—linked up to form " jumping-off trenches " in advance of the front line.

5. The construction of assembly trenches.

Defensive Preparations.

1. New lines of barbed wire, behind which occasional traverses and dugouts appear, marking the trace of an intended new line.

2. A general strengthening and deepening of trenches.

3. Additions to existing wire.

4. The rapid marking out and construction of new switch lines.

5. An increase in the number of battery positions.

During Actual Operations.

Important points to be looked for :—

1. Tracks leading into shell holes containing detached parties and machine guns.

2. Old battery positions, which are often wired round and converted into strong points.

3. Blocks and barricades in communication trenches.

4. Craters in roads—generally anti-tank.

5. New tracks across country.

6. New active battery positions.

OBSERVATION EXERCISES

EXERCISE 1.

In all Exercises the distance to objects seen will be judged and the estimates entered in Observation Reports.

Locality.

Position of Observers.

Exercise.

To train men in observation by progressive stages.

1. All inanimate objects to be found in or near a front-line trench or wherever troops may be congregated.

2. Concealed objects—

2 steel helmets	1 pick
2 rifles	1 shovel
2 old boots	1 broken pick helve
1 telescope	1 respirator
1 telescope case	1 coat
1 bayonet	1 dummy head
1 scabbard	1 long screw picket
1 S.D. cap	1 shovel haft.

3. Kit required :—
   Telescopes, notebooks, pencils, ground sheets, watch, walking sticks (if available).

4. Opening talk—
   (a) Class to work in pairs, one observer, one writer, and change round.
   (b) Objects are things one would expect to see in war.
   (c) Objects all within ... yds.
   (d) Arc to watch.
   (e) What seen, when and where to be entered in proper Observation Report.
   (f) When an object is found, take glass off it and get on to it again quickly for practice.

5. Demonstration of proper way to use a telescope :—
   (a) On back, comfortable.
   (b) On face, comfortable and concealed.
   (c) Back to back with observer, rested.
   (d) Using a stick for support—
              (i) Standing.
             (ii) Kneeling.
            (iii) Sitting.
   (e) Round a tree, out of sight.

6. Class observes with naked eye.

7. Class observes with telescopes.

8. Collection of reports and objects, and discussion.

9. Timing :—

Talk and demonstration	...	...	10 min.	
Naked eye	...	...	...	...	5 min.
Telescopes	...	...	...	...	25 min.
Discussion and collection of reports	...	5 min.	

45 min.

EXERCISE 2.

Locality.

Position.

Exercise.

1. To try to locate men as follows :—
    (*a*) Concealed men using natural cover and no camouflage coverings.
    (*b*) Twelve concealed men with rifles.

2. Kit required : As for Exercise 1.

3. Opening Talk : As for Exercise 1, but men used and all within .... yds.

4. Class observes with naked eye.

5. Telescopes.

6. Discussion and collection of reports.

7. Timing :

Talk	...	...	...	5 min.
Naked eye		...	...	5 min.
Telescopes		...	...	30 min.
Discussion		...	...	5 min.

45 min.

EXERCISE 3.

Locality.

Position of Observers.

Exercise.

1. To try to spot—
    (*a*) Concealed men using camouflage.
    (*b*) Twelve men.

2. Kit required : As for Exercise 1.

3. Opening talk : As for Exercise 2.

4. Class observes with naked eye. As for Exercise 2.

5. Telescopes. As for Exercise 2.

6. Discussion. As for Exercise 2.

7. Timing. As for Exercise 2.

NOTE.—Movement and sound introduced twenty minutes after start of observing with telescopes. Signal flag to control.
Field-glasses for comparison.

45 minutes.

EXERCISE 4.

Locality.

Position of Observers.

Exercise.

1. Long-distance observation—
    (a) Introducing movement simulating action of enemy scouts.
    (b) Objects : 3 or 4 scouts.

2. Kit required : As for Exercise 1.

3. Talk : As for Exercise 2, but students to draw panorama sketch and accurate pin-pointing from map in Observation Reports.

4. Class observes with telescopes.

5. Discussion.

6. Timing :—
    Introductory and panorama sketch ... ... ½ hour.
    Telescopes ... ... 2 hours.

NOTE.—For purposes of training a certain amount of movement will purposely be made fairly obvious.

Signal flag to control.

EXERCISE 5.

Locality.

Position of Observers.

Exercise.

1. Close scrutiny of trench system.

2. Objects : N.C.O. Instructor and fatigue men, dummy heads, periscopes, picks, shovels, rifles, camouflage, bombs, Very lights.

3. Kit required : As for Exercise 1.

4. Opening talk, stressing patience.

5. Class observes with telescopes.

6. Discussion.

7. Timing :—

Introduction	...	...	...	5 min.	
Sketch of trench		...	...	} 80 min.	} 1½ hrs.
Telescopes	...	...	...		
Discussion	...	...	...	5 min.	

NOTE.—Signal flag to control.

Object.

Close scrutiny of a trench system. Distance between trenches, 150 yds.

175

Method.

Students acting as observers occupy if possible short section of a prepared trench.

N.C.O. Instructor and fatigue men occupy the trenches and carry out the following :—

1. Rifles in loopholes moved with caution.

2. Rifles in loopholes moved carelessly.

3. Rifles pushed through loopholes and sand from discharge blown up in front.

4. Looking over parapet with telescopes.

5. Looking through observation post with telescopes.

6. Putting up smoke to represent cooking.

7. Signal up working party. Party arrive and expose tools they are carrying.

8. Working party throwing up earth, etc.

9. Moving sandbags very carefully on top of parapet.

10. Looking over parapet with periscope, cautiously.

11. Looking over parapet camouflaged with sandbags.

12. Exposing periscopes incautiously.

13. Looking through observation posts with curtains raised and smoke filtering through.

14. Walking the dummy.

15. Throwing bombs.

The above take place at **irregular** intervals during the time allotted (*i.e.*, 1½ hrs.). Long intervals, short exposures.

EXERCISE 6.

Locality.

Position of Observers.

Exercise.

1. Introducing long distance (1,000 yds.) Reconnaissance and Use of Fieldcraft by trained Scout Instructors, who will attempt to approach Student Observers unseen—simulating enemy reconnaissance patrol.

2. Objects : Instructors and trained Scout Instructors.

3. Kit required : As for Exercise 1.

4. Introductory, but students to draw panorama sketch and accurate pin-pointing on map in Observation Reports.

5. Class observes with telescopes.

6. Discussion.

7. Timing :—

Introductory and sketch	...	½ hr.	⎫
Telescopes	...	1½ hrs.	⎬ 2 hrs.
Signal flag to control.			⎭

PATROLLING EXERCISES

SCOUTING, PATROLLING, ETC.

FIRST PERIOD.

Exercise 1. Individual Stalking.

Locality.

Object.—To teach the use of ground and cover.

1. Demonstration by Instructor of how to crawl.

(*a*) Forwards
(*b*) Backwards   }   TIME : 10 MINUTES.
(*c*) Sideways

Applies to snipers and scouts.

2. Demonstration by Instructor of how to move unseen without crawling.

Applies to snipers and scouts. TIME : 10 MINUTES.

3. Demonstration by four Instructors of how to get out of a trench and take up diamond formation.

Applies chiefly to scouts. TIME : 20 MINUTES.

4. Demonstration of formations by Instructor and students.

Applies to scouts. TIME : 5 MINUTES.

TOTAL TIME : 45 MINUTES.

STEALTH PATROL EXERCISE (DAY).

Locality.

Object.—To show how an unwary observer, sniper or sentry may be caught napping and pounced on by three or four resolute men.

This is done by Instructors—

(*a*) On a man lying out in the open.

(*b*) On a man in a listening post or shell-hole.

NOTE.—This demonstration is shown by day, but will more usually only be feasible at night.

TIME : ½ HOUR.

SECOND PERIOD.

Stalking.

Syndicates practise Crawling.

Object.—Students to get as close as possible to each other unseen.

Procedure.—Five syndicates of six each. In each syndicate two students at a time stalk each other. First one to see the other raises hand. Remainder watch.

POINTS FOR SYNDICATE INSTRUCTORS.

1. Each stalk very short—about 50 yds.

2. Keep spectators well away from stalkers.

3. Students must stop, look and listen during stalk.

4. Time allowed for each complete stalk and discussion, 15 minutes—*i.e.*, each syndicate, six students ; each stalk, two students, 15 minutes. Thus whole syndicate exercised in 45 minutes.

THIRD PERIOD.

Syndicates practise Approach and Kill. (The sniper at work.)

Procedure.—Syndicate as above, but only one student at a time in each will stalk a flagged enemy sniper. Remainder watch.

POINTS FOR SYNDICATE INSTRUCTORS.

1. The sniper must be able to see the flag before he starts and must be lying down.

2. Half the syndicate sent to flag and act as observers. Must lie down before start of stalk.

3. Remainder watch sniper ; must keep well away from him, instructor likewise.

4. Distance from starting-point, 400 yds. approximately.

5. Distance for kill, maximum 200 yds., preferably 100 yds. Reason, need for **certain** death.

6. During stalk say nothing, but if too slow altogether quicken up.

7. Remember the sniper is out to get his man and can take as long as he likes over it. But he should not waste time by crawling slowly over easy or dead ground when sooner or later he is sure to come to difficult ground where he will have to.

8. Remember that the easier the ground for the stalker (*i.e.*, dead ground), the more likely he is to lose the mark. Hence need for observation *en route*, also in case the mark moves off.

9. At end, ask observers at flag if they saw anything ; criticize stalk.

N.B.—Make sure the sniper can shoot to kill from final position chosen.

10. If risks **have** to be taken, take them early.

Then change syndicate round, sending those who observed from the flag to watch the sniper and *vice versa*, and repeat as before.

TIME ALLOTTED : 1½ HOURS, during which it should be possible to exercise two students in each syndicate, each stalk and discussion taking 45 minutes—*i.e.*, ten students exercised in all, remainder having watched from sniper's end and enemy's end.

KIT REQUIRED : Five different-coloured flags.

RECONNAISSANCE PATROL EXERCISE (DAYLIGHT).

Locality.—HUNTLEY—PODWELL GRANGE area.

NOTE.—A special daylight reconnaissance ; carried out by battalion scouts.

Object.—To show, by demonstration given by four Instructors, the action of a Reconnaissance Patrol when definite information is required as quickly as possible. Students will watch.

For the purpose of this scheme built-up areas should be ignored if they interfere with tactical dispositions, the whole idea of the scheme being to concentrate on patrolling, and the ground chosen is selected for that purpose only.

Verbal Orders given to Patrol Leader by Battalion Intelligence Officer.

Information.

1. Yesterday we drove back the enemy. From air reports it is believed that they are now holding the high ground PODWELL GRANGE—CHERRY TREE HOUSE.

2. Our F.D.Ls. are now occupying the high ground BUNHILL HALL—ST. STEPHEN'S SPINNEY.

Intention.

3. You will find out whether or not the enemy are occupying PODWELL GRANGE.

Method.

4. The patrol will consist of yourself and three men.

5. You, Corporal Snooks, will lead the patrol.

6. Private Smith will be second-in-command.

7. You will leave at .... hours.

8. Your first bound will be Road Junction 580521.

[NOTE.—Preliminary reconnaissance by Battalion Intelligence Officer and Patrol Leader has already been carried out. For the purpose of this scheme the first bound will be considered as the starting-point.]

179

9. You will keep South of the HUNTLEY—WILLERSLEY road.

10. The C.O. wants this information as quickly as possible. I am not going to tie you down, but remember speed is important.

11. Get the information without the enemy knowing that you have got it.

Administrative.

12. You will not carry rifles ; you will not wear equipment, steel helmets or gas masks.

13. You will carry revolvers, if available, two Mills grenades in your pockets. Balaclava helmets will be worn, and you will carry field-glasses.

14. You will dirty your face and hands.

15. You will leave behind anything that shines, all badges and papers.
[Note.—The patrol has already been fed, but will have a hot drink on return.]

Intercommunication.

16. The password is STAR. A word difficult for the Huns to pronounce is preferable.

17. No other patrols will be out.

18. You will arrange beforehand any signs or signals you require.

19. Battalion H.Q. is at GRANT'S FARM 598641.

20. Company H.Q. is at Road and Track Junction 584526, where you will report on return. I. Sec. N.C.O. will be there.

21. ANY QUESTIONS ?

TIME : ¾ HOUR.

Cutting Wire.

Students will be shown how to cut concertina wire at PODWELL GRANGE—

(a) By two men.

(b) By one man.

Points.

1. Near ground.

2. Lying on back.

3. Wire held to stop spring-back and noise.

4. If alone, cut near post.

Orders given by Patrol Leader to His Patrol.

On receipt of his orders from the Intelligence Officer, the Patrol Leader will say :—

Information.

1. Air reports the enemy in the vicinity of PODWELL GRANGE.

2. You know where our Company H.Q. is.

Intention.

    3. We are to find out whether or not the enemy are occupying PODWELL GRANGE. It's over there, about 1,000 yds. away.

Method.

    4. The C.O. wants this information as quickly as possible.

    5. We are to get it without being seen by the enemy.

    6. We are to keep this side of the HUNTLEY—WILLERSLEY road.

    7. So we will make for that ridge first of all and have a look. You, Sergeants Davidson and Ross, will work up round the left flank towards those trees and have a look over the shoulder from there. One of you keep me in sight. Sergeant McLennan and I will go round the right flank by those houses and have a look over the shoulder from there. Then we will see what happens.

Administrative.

    8. We'll go just as we are—I mean Battle Dress and stocking-caps. Dirty your faces and hands ; no badges or papers ; bring your field-glasses and scrounge revolvers if you can. Put a couple of Mills bombs in your pocket.

Intercommunication.

    9. The password is STAR.

    10. No other patrols will be out.

    11. If you see anyone give us a wave.

    12. When we get back we've got to report to Company H.Q.

    13. ANY QUESTIONS ?

REQUIRED.—Four men with rifles, and Staff Sergeant to represent enemy ; ten rounds blank.

RECONNAISSANCE PATROL EXERCISE (NIGHT).

Low-power field-glasses required if suitable night to show usefulness at night.

In contrast to the Reconnaissance Patrol Scheme by day, here a very tricky job is to be done and accurate information required, which can only be done with extreme caution. Speed is, therefore, not of primary importance.

NOTE.—On getting near the enemy's wire, one man, or at most two men, will crawl forward the last few yards. During the repetition of this scheme, one patrol will be sent out from each of the opposing trench systems simultaneously. Object : To teach that a Reconnaissance Patrol should avoid fighting, if possible, but always be prepared to.

Locality.

Object.—To develop night sense and apply to night conditions lessons already learnt in the daytime.

Procedure.—A trench-to-trench crawl carried out by four students at a time, who must leave their own trench, crawl through their own wire, up to the enemy's wire and tie pieces of flannelette on it, and return to their own trench unseen and unheard. All remaining students stay in trench to represent enemy, and when they see or hear anything a Very light will be fired.

Distance between trenches, about 130 yds. It is hoped to be able to carry out two patrols in three hours.

Demonstration.

Demonstration given of what to do and what not to do when a Very light goes up :

> { (a) By standing still.
> { (b) By lying down before flare lights up.

> { (c) By movement, betraying position.
> { (d) By looking up, betraying position.

The above is repeated, when another two patrols should be exercised. TIME : 3 HOURS.

It is hoped that twenty students will thus be exercised altogether.

FIGHTING PATROL EXERCISE (DAY).

Locality.—Flag needed (to control).

Object.—This is a tactical scheme run as a demonstration to bring out particularly the action of battalion scouts acting as guides to a Fighting Patrol and snipers working in conjunction with a Fighting Patrol but independent of it. The scheme will be frequently halted and everyone will stand up and see what everyone else is doing. It also shows how snipers can cover patrol during approach march, and particularly how, by lying up after the patrol has withdrawn, they can deal with any enemy who come to investigate.

TIME : 1½ HOURS.

Details of Scheme.
Information.

1. Enemy are using cottage in No Man's Land as an assembly area for patrols. It is not strongly held.

2. We are a Fighting Patrol. We have two battalion scouts to guide us, and two snipers will work in conjunction with us but independent of us.

Intention.

3. We are going to make a dawn raid and mop it up.

Method.

4. Starting-point—tree 100 yds. E. of JOHNSON'S FARM.

5. Two scouts will guide patrol.

182

6. Two snipers will work on flanks, keeping level with scouts.

7. On nearing cottage, patrol will be halted ; leader will confer with scouts and make his plan.

8. Patrol withdraws. Snipers lie up.

NOTE.—The approach march should be taken as being made during semi-darkness, the final assault at the change of night to day, and the withdrawal before full daylight. Formations would thus have to be varied, but the used ones (*i.e.*, daylight) are for demonstration purposes.

Fighting Patrol by Day.

On receipt of orders from Company Commander, Patrol Leader will say :—

Information.

1. The enemy are using the cottage in No Man's Land as an assembly area for patrols ; it is not strongly held.

2. You know where Company H.Q. is. (JOHNSON'S FARM.)

3. We are going to raid the cottage and capture prisoners and get identifications.

Method.

4. The patrol will consist of twenty-two.

5. Formation : Diamond, in four groups ; distances and intervals, about 25 yds., each man 5 yds. from the next man. Scouts, within sight in front and on flanks ; Thompson guns, one with leading group and one with rear.

6. Sergeant Smith second-in-command.

7. Two snipers, one on either flank, will cover advance, acting independently.

8. We leave at .... hours.

9. Starting-point (pointing).
   [NOTE.—Preliminary reconnaissance has been carried out by leader.]

10. We must get there unseen.

11. We must get back as soon as possible.

Administrative.

12. You will carry rifles with bayonets fixed, magazines loaded with five rounds, ten rounds in the pocket, two Mills grenades, and will wear steel helmets.

13. You will not wear gas masks or equipment.

14. You will take with you two Thompson guns and three spare magazines a gun.

15. No badges or papers.

Intercommunication.

16. Password is VANCOUVER.

17. No other patrols will be out.

18. We are to report to Company H.Q. on return. (JOHNSON'S FARM.)

19. ANY QUESTIONS ?

Orders for Snipers by Intelligence Officer.

1. To keep on flanks of patrol during approach and cover advance.

2. To get in position to cover house during assault, particularly to deal with any enemy running away from it.

3. To push on to close vicinity of house and lie up and cover approaches to it, particularly to deal with any enemy coming to investigate or collect wounded after raid is over.

FIGHTING PATROL (DAYLIGHT).

A DAWN RAID.

Object.—To show the action of scouts and snipers (as already explained) and also patrol formation.

Procedure—1. STARTING-POINT.—Two scouts go out, one some distance behind the other, to cover the advance. Patrol Leader follows rear scout, also some distance behind him (within sight). Flank scouts act as flank guards, and rear scouts as rear guards, all within sight. Patrol follows leader in formation about 50 yds. in rear of him. Patrol formation—diamond ; intervals and distances about 25 yds. Intervals and distances of each man in each group about 5 yds. Leading scout halts on arrival at dangerous area ; second scout sees him signal and goes to him. Patrol leader comes up. All halt and lie down. Leader makes reconnaissance and plan.

N.B.—During this advance the snipers have been well out on the flanks about 100 yds. from the patrol and just ahead of the main body of the patrol, working on their own.

2. THE ASSAULT.—No. 1 Group in single file, and singly and keeping low, to go round right flank. Right sniper, who has already found his position, will cover them. No. 2 Group to go round left flank. Left sniper, who has already found his position, will cover them. Leader, with Nos. 3 and 4 Groups, also round by the right. Two Thompson guns get ready for frontal covering fire. On whistle signal, all close in together. After raid, Nos. 1 and 2 withdraw by whistle signal, covered by Thompson guns. Whole patrol forms up under cover and withdraws.

N.B.—Snipers remain. Right flank will cross road and gain opposite bank to position covering open country behind house, also road. Left flank stays where he is, covering the house. Both have covered lines of withdrawal for use later.

FIGHTING PATROL EXERCISE (NIGHT).

Locality.—BUNHILL HALL—CHERRY TREE FARM area.

Object.—To show the functioning of a Fighting Patrol by night and develop night sense.

For the purposes of this scheme, built-up areas should be ignored if they interfere with tactical dispositions, the whole idea of the scheme being to concentrate on patrolling ; the ground chosen is selected for that purpose only.

NOTE.—A Platoon of men will be the enemy. Five rounds blank per man and fireworks.

Verbal Orders given by Company Commander to Patrol Leader.

Information.

1. The enemy are holding the general line STANTON—EAST-HAMPTON—TONBY. The Battalion Intelligence Officer reports that the enemy is occupying CHERRY TREE FARM, possibly as an assembly area for patrols, at any rate during the hours of darkness. It does not appear to be a strongly defended locality.

2. Our troops are holding the general line TOPTON RISE—STOREY HOUSE—STEEN HOUSE. (Company is occupying F.D.Ls. about the A of ARTINGHAM ROAD 611544, with two platoons astride the HUNTLEY—SPURLING railway at road and rail crossing 587523 and 611561.)

Intention.

3. You will raid CHERRY TREE FARM and bring back prisoners and identifications.

Method.

4. The patrol will consist of yourself and twenty-one other ranks.

5. You have seen the ground—watch your formation.

6. You, Lieutenant Smith, will lead the patrol.

7. You, Sergeant Brown, will be second-in-command.

8. You will leave at 2300 hours.

   [NOTE.—Preliminary reconnaissance has been carried out in daylight by Patrol Leader, and section commanders have had the lie of the land pointed out to them.]

9. Get back before it is light.

10. You will start from Road and Track Junction 582529. Your second bound will be TEALD 575528.

11. You will overcome any enemy resistance encountered before reaching your objective.

Administrative.

12. You will carry rifles, with bayonets fixed, magazines loaded with five rounds, ten rounds in the pocket and two Mills grenades. Wire-cutters.

13. You will not wear gas masks, equipment or steel helmets.

14. You will take with you two Thompson guns and three magazines per gun.

15. You will leave behind anything that shines, luminous watches, badges and papers.

16. You will have a hot meal at 2000 hrs., and you will have a hot drink on return.

Intercommunication.

17. The password is STAR. A word difficult for the Huns to pronounce is preferable.

18. No other patrols will be out.

19. You will arrange beforehand any signs or signals you may require.

20. Company H.Q. is at 601534, where you will report on return.

21. ANY QUESTIONS ?

TIME : 3 HOURS.

SUGGESTED FORMATION FOR A NIGHT FIGHTING PATROL.

Strength : 22, composed as under :—

1 Officer.
1 N.C.O.
6 Scouts from Intelligence Section.
14 Men.

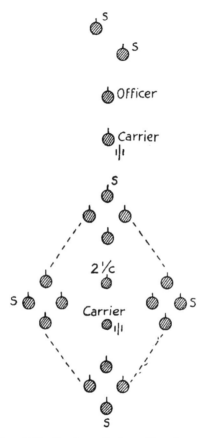

NOTE.—If available, Scouts on flanks could each carry Thompson guns.

When advancing in file, the 2 i/c and Tommy gun would drop to the rear of the patrol.

Fighting Patrol (Night).

On receipt of orders from Company Commander, Patrol Leader will say :—

Information.

1. The enemy are occupying CHERRY TREE FARM, possibly as an assembly area for patrols, at any rate during the hours of darkness. It does not appear to be strongly held.

2. You know where Company H.Q. is.

Intention.

3. We are going to raid CHERRY TREE FARM and bring back prisoners or identifications—*i.e.*, alive or dead.

Method.

4. The patrol will consist of 22.

5. Formations : To begin with, file, all closed up, two scouts in front and two behind, all within sight of each other. On reaching the open, diamond, four groups, but each man practically touching his neighbour. Thompson guns—one with leading group, one with rear.

6. Sergeant Smith second-in-command.

7. We are leaving at .... hours.
   [NOTE.—Preliminary reconnaissance has been carried out in daylight and section commanders know lie of land.]

8. We are to get back before it is light.

9. We start from Road and Track Junction 582529.

10. Our second bound will be TEALD 575528.

11. We will overcome any enemy resistance encountered before reaching our objective.

Administrative.

12. You will carry rifles with bayonets fixed, magazines loaded with five rounds, ten rounds in pocket, and two Mills grenades.

13. You will not wear gas masks, equipment or steel helmets.

14. You will take with you two Thompson guns and three magazines a gun.

15. You will leave behind anything that shines, luminous watches, badges and papers.

Intercommunication.

16. The password is STAR.

17. No other patrols will be out.

18. Company H.Q. is at 611544, where we will report on return.

19. ANY QUESTIONS ?

FIGHTING PATROL (NIGHT).

A NIGHT RAID.

Appreciation of the Situation.

The enemy are known to be holding CHERRY TREE FARM, but not strongly, and as only during the hours of darkness for certain, it is suspected that this is an assembly area for their patrols. Therefore, in all probability we would only expect to find sentries posted in the close vicinity of the buildings. Great care, however, must be taken all the way in case an enemy patrol is already out or on the point of starting. In the latter event, as is the habit of such patrols when leaving isolated buildings, we might expect to bump into a party of three or more scouts put out fanwise to act as a covering party while the patrol is forming up.

Suggested Procedure.

1. FROM THE STARTING-POINT.—The patrol should proceed in close formation, leader and scouts in front in single file within sight of each other, remainder in Groups 1, 2, 3, 4 behind, also in file, all closed up ; two scouts bringing up rear and in sight of last group. Thompson guns between second leading scout and No. 1 Group and between No. 4 Group and leading rearguard scout. This formation used for going along a path or track. On reaching top, proper diamond formation adopted and maintained thereafter. Greatest care in forming up ; cover it with Thompson gun.

During the whole advance the patrol, led and controlled by the leader, must move forward short distances only at a time and halt frequently and listen. If a dark night, everyone in the patrol must be within touching distance. If moonlight, more open formation and when halted at any rate kneel.

N.B.—At night remember background and always keep in the hollows ; they can't see you and you can see more looking up from hollows on to ridges, etc.

2. Should the patrol proceed without incident to a point approximately, say, 100 yds. from the objective (as in all probability they would be able to if properly led and handled), they should then halt and keep down. If a noisy approach gives them away, it will be a case of going for the enemy on sight without any special prearranged plan.

3. THE ASSAULT.—If the approach march is successfully completed, surprise will then be the first consideration, so keep dead still and quiet, and listen for a few minutes. If nothing heard, two scouts in single file and within touching distance on hands and knees get as close as possible and try to find out whether house is occupied or not while patrol waits and listens. They hear voices and return to the patrol. Leader makes his plan : Nos. 1, 2 and 3 Groups will attack simultaneously from one flank, while No. 4 Group remains in reserve where it is to cover. Patrol take one Thompson gun, the other stays with No. 4. The patrol moves silently out to the flank.

189

They should aim at getting well within 50 yds. Then, on given whistle signal (prearranged), all close in quickly together simultaneously.

If the enemy makes no sound, you might send a couple of men round one flank to make a noise purposely and attract attention. The noise they make could be the signal for you to assault from the opposite flank.

If it is a **very** dark night (which is not suitable), the principle is don't get your men scattered ; this will only lead to confusion and casualties.

If a **fairly** dark night, an alternative would be to try to partially surround the house before delivering the assault.

Anyone who can get a prisoner, grab him at once and take him to the covering group, being careful to shout out the password. Remember the bayonet is far safer than the bullet or the bomb. If enemy resistance is weak, mop them all up ; if strong, on given signal (three whistle blasts) get out of it quickly. Bring back own wounded. Withdraw in direction of covering group, who are all ready to cover them if pursued. Covering group will then cover withdrawal of remainder. Patrol must be collected together as soon as possible to see none left behind. Then straight for home.

Enemy Defence Platoon.

Will occupy CHERRY TREE FARMHOUSE. Will not actually enter buildings, but get as close as possible to them. Will post sentry groups (three or four) to cover danger points. These must be fairly close to buildings, hidden in hedges, etc. Main body assumed to be getting ready to go out on patrol, a certain amount of noise going on, talking and movement, sufficient to betray their presence ; in other words, they are quite unsuspecting and are relying on their sentries.

When the assault takes place, the enemy should get right amongst them so there will be a wild scramble. Any man overpowered by two to one and told " Hands up !" is definitely a prisoner and must go quickly and quietly. The remainder will be withdrawn on signal by O.C. Defence Platoon.

NOTE.—The object is for the enemy patrol to get prisoners and identifications, and once this has been done we don't want the thing to turn into a running dog-fight or a brawl.

N.B.—For safety's sake, neither side will fix bayonets.

RECONNAISSANCE EXERCISE (DAYLIGHT).

Locality.—SPURLING PARK.

Notes.—A special daylight reconnaissance carried out by battalion scouts in country not unlike certain sectors of No Man's Land on the Western Front.

Object.—To show by demonstration, given by four Instructors, the action of a Reconnaissance Patrol when definite information about the exact disposition of the enemy's F.D.Ls. is required.

Verbal Orders given to the Patrol Leader by the Battalion Intelligence Officer.

Information.

1. The enemy are holding the general line HURSTHILL PHEASANTRY—East edge of CALNE WOOD—CHERRY TREE HOUSE.

   Our F.D.Ls. are occupying the high ground (inclusive)) SWEET BRIAR PLANTATION—(Exclusive) POLLARD WOOD.

Narrative.

2. The dispositions made by the enemy function as follows :—

    (i) By the use of anti-tank obstacles, in this case woods, to offer a threat to the enemy's tanks—*i.e.*, to defy them to enter these localities, thus forcing them into the gaps in between where A/T guns and mines are sited.

    (ii) By keeping the infantry back from the forward slopes where they would inevitably be shelled to bits, and by putting them into the A/T obstacles, they can obviously only be tackled by infantry. Their trenches are sited some way back in the woods, where they would not be shelled, where they would be very hard to see even from the air, and even their wire would be pretty well hidden.

    (iii) By having O.Ps. out in front, and particularly on the flanks, in daytime, and by constant patrolling at night, to prevent enemy assembling for attack in No Man's Land and give warning if they are.

    In order to prove the enemy defences, observation is essential. In daylight, trained scouts can effectively do this ; at night, patrols, who can at any rate draw the enemy's fire.

    The need for accurately pin-pointing the enemy's F.D.Ls. prior to any attack or raid by patrols is obvious.

Intention.

3. You will find out the exact dispositions of the enemy's F.D.Ls. between (inclusive) stream running from PHEASANTRY to small pond 569537 and (inclusive) stream running from East corner of CALNE WOOD to Lake 571565.

Method.

4. The patrol will consist of yourself and three men.

5. You, Corporal Snooks, will lead the patrol.

6. Private Smith will be second-in-command.

7. You will leave at .... hours.

8. Your first bound will be fence and track junction 580547.

   [NOTE.—Preliminary reconnaissance by Battalion I.O. and Patrol Leader has already been carried out.

   For the purpose of this scheme the first bound will be considered as the starting-point.]

Administrative.

9. You will not carry rifles ; you will not wear equipment, steel helmets or gas masks.

10. You will carry revolvers, if available, two Mills grenades in your pockets. Balaclava helmets will be worn and you will carry field-glasses.

11. You will dirty your face and hands.

12. You will leave behind anything that shines, all badges and papers.

   [NOTE.—The patrol has already been fed, but will have a hot drink on return.]

Intercommunication.

13. The password is STAR ; a word difficult for the Boche to pronounce is preferable.

14. No other patrols will be out.

15. You will arrange beforehand any signs or signals you may require.

16. Battalion H.Q. is at SAND PIT 587551.

17. Company H.Q. is at SPURLING FARM 575549, where you will report on return. I. Sec. N.C.O. will be there.

18. ANY QUESTIONS ?

KIT REQUIRED.—Four pairs field-glasses ; four men with rifles for enemy F.D.Ls.

TIME : 1¼ HOURS.

Orders given by Patrol Leader to his Patrol.

On receipt of his orders from the Intelligence Officer, the Patrol Leader will say :—

Information.

1. The enemy are holding the line PHEASANTRY and CHERRY TREE HOUSE (pointing).

2. You know where our Company H.Q. is.

Intention.

3. We are to find out the exact dispositions of the enemy's F.D.Ls. between those two streams (pointing).

Method.

4. Our first position to observe from will be just in front there (pointing).

5. (After looking) That wood on the left seems a good place to have a look from, but the enemy may have an O.P. in it so we must be careful. Sergeant Ross and I will go and have a look from there. I'll go in front. Sergeant Ross, keep me in sight. Follow me and do as I do. Sergeants Davidson and McLennan, you go round by the right and try and get observation from somewhere about that little copse.

Administrative.

6. We'll go just as we are—I mean Battle Dress and stocking-caps. Dirty your face and hands ; no badges or papers. Bring your field-glasses, and scrounge revolvers if you can. Put a couple of Mills bombs in your pocket.

Intercommunication.

7. The password is STAR.

8. No other patrols will be out.

9. When we get back we've got to report to Company H.Q.

10. ANY QUESTIONS ?

Procedure.

1. For this demonstration the two scouts on the right start first ; students follow. Sergeant Davidson, who leads, says to Sergeant McLennan : " Keep me in sight and follow me and do as I do."

On reaching the corner, Sergeant Davidson creeps carefully round and uses his glasses. Thinks he sees someone on the bridge, creeps round the corner under cover again, calls up Sergeant McLennan, who also has a look. They both agree that they must try somewhere else, so they go back to their starting-point and then go up ditch in middle, thence to dovecot, thence up tree.

LESSONS.

(*a*) Observation posts chosen from starting-point are apt sometimes to prove disappointing when you get to them, however well trained you are.

(*b*) Observation post chosen affords good observation, covered approach and cover from view and to some extent from fire.

2. Then scouts on left make for LOWHILL, being very careful in case of enemy observation point. On finding it useless, turn back and, using ditch, make for clump of gorse.

LESSONS.

As before ; in addition, daylight reconnaissance **is** possible and very useful if ground and cover properly used.

SNIPER COURSE

SHOOTING PRACTICES.

No. of Prac-tice	Range	Conditions of Practice	No. of Rounds	H.P.S.
1	Yds. 100	GROUPING. Aperture sight. Target : 4 ft. white screen with 4 in. black rectangle. A. Zeroing ; 5 rounds. B. Check zero and score 5 rounds.	5 5	Nil 30
2	100	As for Practice 1, using telescopic sights.	10	30
3	200	APPLICATION. Aperture sights. Target : 4 ft. with 9 in. aiming mark ; 5 in. bull, 7 in. inner, 9 in. outer. 2 Sighting shots and 5 to count.	7	20
4	200	As for Practice 3, using telescopic sights.	7	20
5	200	SNAPSHOOTING. Target : Fig. 5 with inscribed ovals ; 5 × 3 in. bull, 7 × 5 in. inner ; remainder of target outer. A. Aperture sights. B. Telescopic sights. To be fired consecutively. Exposure : 5 of 3 secs. each clear.	5 5	20 20
6	200	MOVING TARGET. Aperture or telescopic sights. Target : Fig. 6 carried at walking pace. Five exposures over a frontage of 15 yds. Each exposure 5 secs.	5	20
7	300	APPLICATION. Telescopic sights. Target : 4 ft. with 12 in. aiming mark ; 7 in. bull, 9 in. inner, 12 in. outer. 2 Sighting shots and 5 to count.	7	20

No. of Practice	Range	Conditions of Practice	No. of Rounds	H.P.S.
8	Yds. 500	APPLICATION. Telescopic sights. Target: 6 ft. with 17 in. aiming mark: 15 in. bull, 18 in. inner, 21 in. outer. 2 Sighting shots and 5 to count.	7	20
9	200	SNAPSHOOTING. Telescopic sights. Target: Special loophole. Targets exposed in loopholes for a period of 5 seconds clear; five exposures. Same target **may** appear twice. Up slow, down sharp. N.B.—" Spotting the Sniper " during this practice.	5	20
10	200 approx.	SNAPSHOOTING. Telescopic sights. Targets: Five Fig. 5's exposed over a given area. Each Fig. exposed for 5 clear seconds. Same Fig. may be exposed twice. Firer in open. (Sling may be used.)	5	20
11	200 approx.	SNAPSHOOTING. Telescopic sights. As for Practice 10, but firing from loophole position.	5	20
12	500 approx.	SNAPSHOOTING. Telescopic sights. Targets: Five Figs. 4A. Conditions as for Practice 10.	5	20
		Grand Totals ...	83	280

NOTES.

Rifle when rested must be rested near the point of balance.

Scoring for Grouping :

1½ in. group	30 points.	4 in. group	15 points.
2 in. ,,	25 ,.	5 in. ,,	10 ,,
3 in. ,,	20 ,,	6 in. ,,	5 ,,

Application : Bull 4 points, inner 3 points, outer 1 point.

Snapshooting : Centre oval 4 points, inner 3 points, rest of target 1 point.

All other Practices : Hit anywhere counts 4 points.

Whenever firing, except during Grouping Practices, an observer with telescope will spot for the firer.

SUGGESTED PROGRAMME FOR SNIPING, SCOUTING, AND OBSERVATION INSTRUCTION
Periods and Detail of Work.

Day of Course	0830—0915	0915—1000	1000—1045	1100—1145	1145—1230	1230—1315	1430—1515	1515—1600
			COURSE ASSEMBLES					
1	0800 Squadding, issue of kit, etc.	Opening Address	Lecture: Care of Arms	Aiming Instruction	Zeroing	Mechanism, Parallax, etc.	Judging Distance 1	Elevation and Thermometer Target
2	Lecture: Firing Point Instruction and Coaching		Range Practice 1 and Coaching			Lecture: Sniping	Judging Distance 2	Aiming off for Wind
3	Lecture: Observation	Range Practice 2 and Coaching				Lecture: Use of Telescope	Lecture: Messages	Lecture: Map Reading. Conventional Signs and Co-ordinates
4	Lecture: Reports and Intelligence Summaries	Range Practices 3 and 4 and Coaching				Observation Objects	Observation Men	Lecture: Camouflage
5	Aiming off for Movement	Range Practices 5 and 6 and Coaching				Lecture: Scouting		

Day of Course	0830—0915	0915—1000	1000—1045	1100—1145	1145—1230	1230—1315	1430—1515	1515—1600
6	Duties of Battalion Intelligence Officer	Range Practices 7 and 8 and Coaching				Lecture: Field Sketching	Observation Camouflage	Field Sketching
7	Lecture: Map Reading, Contours	Observation Exercise 4. Movement in the Open, including Route Report				Lecture: Use of Compass	Individual Stalks and Use of Ground	
8	Compass March		Range Practice 9 and Spotting the Sniper				Individual Stalks and Use of Ground	
9*	Lecture: Patrolling, General	Lecture: Censorship and Handling of Prisoners	Range Practice 10		Lecture: Intelligence, Handing-Over Reports and Summaries	Lecture: Map Reading, Bearings	Observation Close scrutiny of trench.	Stealth Patrol
10	Field Sketching	Range Practice 11			Lecture: Map Reading, Scales	Lecture: Sniping in Open and Trench Warfare	Stealth Patrol	
11	Lecture: Reconnaissance, General	Lecture: Reconnaissance Patrol	Reconnaissance Patrol					

* 2030: Sounds by night.

Periods and Detail of Work—*continued.*

Day of Course	0830—0915	0915—1000	1000—1045	1100—1145	1145—1230	1230—1315	1430—1515	1515—1600
12	Lecture : Snipers' Hides and Loopholes	Range Practice 12		Building loopholes	Building loopholes	Lecture : Battalion Intelligence Section in Attack in Trench Warfare	2030 : Compass march	
13	Lecture : Fighting Patrol	Fighting Patrol by day		Lecture : Front Line and General Intelligence	Lecture : Night Sniping	Lecture : Intelligence, Aeroplane Photos	Reconnaissance Patrol Trench Crawl	
14	Observation Exercise 6 Movement in the open				Reconnaissance Patrol		Fighting Patrol by night	
15	Patrolling Observation and Sniping Exercise							
16	Tommy Gun and Revision	Examination	Discussion					

COURSE DISPERSES

TRAINING SYLLABI

COURSE FOR STAFF CAPTAINS (INTELLIGENCE), BATTALION INTELLIGENCE OFFICERS, AND SCOUTS, OBSERVERS AND SNIPERS.

1st day   0900—1200   Opening remarks. Read and explain Standing Orders. Arrange Class in syndicates. Call roll.

Examination of rifles and telescopic sights. Range 200 yds.

Preliminary application to adjust obvious defects.

Thorough cleaning of rifles.

            1400—1600   Continue preliminary application with open and telescopic sights.

2nd day   0900—1200   Range 200 yds.

When preliminary zeroing of open and telescopic sights is completed and various adjustments carried out, the Class will fire.

First group of 5 shots with open sights.

Second group of 5 shots with telescopic sights. Careful attention will be paid to the groups.

            1400—1600   Further grouping practice. Groups 4 in., 8 in., and 12 in. These groups will not be scored.

3rd day   0900—1200   Range 200 yds.

FIRST PRACTICE. Grouping.

Aiming mark 6 in. black bullseye.

4 in., 8 in. and 12 in. groups.

20, 10 and 5 points.

Two groups of 5 shots, first with open sights, second with telescopic sights. Best group to score.

            1400—1600   Lecture : " Telescopic Sights, Use and Care of."

            1700   Lecture : " Intelligence."

4th day   0900—1200   Range 200 yds.

SECOND PRACTICE. Application target, 2nd Class F.19. Figure with 6 in. invisible bull.

          Bull   ...   ...   4 points.

          Inner   3   ,,

          Outer   2   ,,

Rounds, 10. Open sights.

            1400—1600   Lecture : " Causes of Inaccuracy in Shooting, and Care of Arms."

| 5th day | 0900—1200 | Range 200 yds. |
| | | THIRD PRACTICE. Application target, 2nd Class. Figure as in Second Practice. |

Bull ... ... 4 points.
Inner ... ... 3 ,,
Outer ... ... 2 ,,

Rounds, 10. Telescopic sights.

| | 1400—1600 | Lecture : " Map Reading, Part I." |
| | 1700 | Map Enlarging. By Class. |

| 6th day | 0900—1000 | Lecture : " Map Reading, Part II." |
| | 1015—1200 | Range 200 yds. |

All inaccurate sights and rifles finally tested by instructor, and if possible adjusted. The Class will then fire.

FOURTH PRACTICE. Final Group.

4 in., 8 in. and 12 in. groups.

20, 10 and 5 points.

One group with open sights, one group with sights optional. Best group to score.

| | 1400—1600 | Lecture : " Observation, Part I." |
| | 1700 | Lecture : " Front Line Intelligence, Part I." |

| 7th day (Sunday) | | Holiday. |

8th day	0900—1030	Lecture : " Reconnaissance and Patrols."
	1045—1200	Map Reading, Part II.
	1400—1600	Judging distance.
	1700	Lecture : " Front Line Intelligence, Part II."

| 9th day | 0900—1200 | Range 200 yds. |
| | | FIFTH PRACTICE. Snap-shooting, Boche head. Stationary. Hit, 4 points ; miss, o. |

Rounds, 10 ; 5 rounds open sights, 5 rounds telescopic sights.

| | 1400—1600 | Scouting, open warfare. |
| | 1700 | Lecture : " Use of Compass and Sextant." |

| 10th day | 0900—1200 | Range 200 yds. |
| | | SIXTH PRACTICE. Snap-shooting, bobbing figure. Exposure 4 seconds, interval 3 seconds. Hit, 4 points ; miss, o. |

Rounds, 10 ; 5 rounds open sights, 5 rounds telescopic sights.

| | 1400—1600 | Lecture : " Reports." |
| | | Night Patrol Exercise. |

| 11th day | All day | Tactical Exercise : Scouting, Open Warfare. Reconnaissance of a position—Locating enemy dispositions—Report on topography —Dead ground—Approaches—Timber— Cover—Contours—Field of fire, etc. |
| | 1700 | Prepare reports in accordance with details of Exercise. |

12th day	0900—1000	Class Officers will collect and tabulate reports and complete their own summaries dealing with previous day's work.
	1015—1200	Lecture : " Military Landscape Sketching," illustrated with sketches on blackboard.
	1400—1600	Compass march.
13th day	0900—1000	Lecture : " Sniping."
	1015—1200	Visibility tests in map reading.
		Half holiday.
		Range practice—optional.
14th day (Sunday)		Holiday.
15th day	0900—1200	Range 200 yds.
		SEVENTH PRACTICE. Target, 2nd Class Figure with 6 in. invisible bull.
		Rounds, 10 ; including 3 sighting shots. Can be converted. Seven shots to count. Possible, 28.
	1400—1600	Map reading. Class to fill in features on contour map specially prepared.
	1700	Aeroplane photos.
16th day	0900—1200	Reconnaissance report and sketch in the field. Scout's position to be determined by resection.
		Describe topography and likely positions for observation posts, machine-gun batteries, strong points, etc.
	1400—1600	Range 200 yds.
		EIGHTH PRACTICE. Snap-shooting. Walking man. Exposure, 10 yds. Hit, 4 points. Rounds, 5. Sights optional.
	1700	Lecture : " Camouflage."
17th day	All day	In the field.
		Observation—Prepared Exercise—To train Class in spotting movement, however slight —Snipers firing—Observation posts in occupation by enemy—Machine-gun positions camouflaged, etc.—Disguised enemy scouts. Followed by demonstration of protective colour and use of dummy heads. Also to train Class in preparing quick sketch and clear report.
	1700	Lecture : " Barr and Stroud Range Finder."
18th day	All day	In the field.
		Observation—Map reading—Magnetic and grid bearings—Practical use of protractor—Resection and pin pointing of positions.
	1700	Check day's work.
		Instructors present to answer any questions and give explanations.

19th day	0900—1030	Map reading. Prepared Contours, Part II.
	1045—1200	Conventional signs.
	1400—1600	Lecture : " Observation, Part II."
20th day	0900—1200	Lecture : " Employment of Battalion Intelligence Section in Attack in Open Warfare," followed by discussion.
	.	Half holiday.
		Range practice—optional.
21st day (Sunday)		Holiday.
22nd day	0900—1200	In the field.
		Map reading—Bearings—Pin pointing, etc.
	1400—1600	Range 200 yds.
		NINTH PRACTICE. Snap-shooting Boche head, stationary. Hit, 4 points.
		Rounds, 10 ; 5 rounds open sights, 5 rounds telescopic sights. Possible, 40.
23rd day	0900—1200	Range 500 yds.
		TENTH PRACTICE. Target, 2nd Class Figure. Bull, 16 in. ring.
		Rounds, 10 ; 7 to score, 3 sighters.
	1400—1600	Lecture : " Interior Economy and Duties of Intelligence Section."
	1700	Lecture : " Intelligence — Identification — Captured Documents."
24th day	0900—1200	Lecture : " Handing - Over Reports and Working Maps."
		Test : Class to prepare sketch or map of enemy's position either from memory, aeroplane photo or log map, together with a Handing-Over Report.
	1400—1600	Map reading. Filling in ground features on prepared contours, Part III.
	1700	Lecture : " Battle of Amiens." Organization of Intelligence System illustrated on enlarged map.
25th day	All day	Tactical Exercise. Scouting in open warfare—Locating enemy—Mapping routes on enlarged map prepared individually by each member of the Class—Writing and forwarding reports—Establishing observation posts and generally keeping touch with the enemy.
	1700	Re-write notes on day's work and hand in to O.C. of Attack and Defence.
26th day	All day	In the field. Exercise—Guiding and map reading tests.
27th day		Final Address.
		Class departs.

INTELLIGENCE COURSE FOR STAFF CAPTAINS (INTELLIGENCE) AND BATTALION INTELLIGENCE OFFICERS.

1st day	0900	Lecture : " Object and Outline of Course." General Lecture on " Intelligence."
	1000	Lecture : " Object and Outline of Scouting and Sniping School Course."
Remainder of morning		Practical work on Corps School range and model trenches, to include practical use of various types of sights.
	1400	Class discussion on Patrols.
	1700	Lecture : " Aeroplane Photographs — Characteristics of various types (vertical, stereoscopic, oblique). General principles of light and shade."
2nd day	0900	Lecture on " Intelligence Organization throughout the Divisions," followed by a general discussion.
	1100	Lecture and discussion on reports and message-writing.
	1400	Training Exercise for a Battalion Intelligence Section on ground. Scheme to be handed in by 0900 on third day.
	1700	Air photographs—General.
3rd day	0900	Lecture : " Intelligence (B), General Organization, C.E. Work and Prevention of Leakage of Information."
	0945	Lecture : " Scope and Outline Intelligence (E), Works Listening Sets ; Leakage of Information by Telephone."
	1100	Discussion : Previous Afternoon's Exercise.
	1400	Lecture : " Identifications and Captured Documents, etc., and German Army."
	1700	Lecture : " General Intelligence."
4th day	0900	Lecture : " Co-operation between Infantry Observation Posts, Artillery Forward Observer Officers and Trench Mortars ; General Outline of Artillery Arrangements for obtaining Gunnery Intelligence and Method of obtaining Action."
	1100	Lecture : " Observation, Co-ordination of Observation, Observation Post Reports." To be followed by Field Work : Observation and Written Reports (to include lecture on and practical use of compass).
	1700	Lecture : " Counter-Battery Work."

5th day	0900	Lecture : " Scouting and Patrolling ; Open Warfare." To be followed by a Tactical Training Exercise of a Battalion Intelligence Section.
	1700	Lecture : " Part Intelligence Organization plays in the Divisional Organization."
6th day	0900	General discussion on past week's work.
	1100	Lecture : " General Points to be considered by Intelligence Officer for Open Warfare."

NOTE.—(a) All exercises carried out on the ground. Reports to be handed in and a general criticism of reports to take place at end of exercises.

(b) Guiding principle throughout all instruction is to impress the fact that intelligence and action go hand-in-hand.

SPECIAL COURSE : OBSERVATION AND SCOUTING—MAP READING FOR SELECTED BATTALION N.C.Os. ONLY.

1st day	0900	Call roll, read Standing Orders and explain. Arrange Class in syndicates. Explain details of Course.
	1115	Lecture : " Observation."
	1400—1600	Judging distances.
	1700	Lecture : " Barr and Stroud Range Finder."
2nd day	0900—1215	Lecture : " Map Reading." Followed by simple tests.
	1400—1600	Lecture : " Compass." Followed by practical test of orientation of maps.
	1700	Lecture : " Identification and Captured Documents."
3rd day	0900—1215	Lecture : " New Military Landscape Sketching." Examples and tests. Half holiday.
4th day	0900—1030	Lecture : " Scouting and Patrolling."
	1045—1215	Lecture : " Reports."
	1400—1600	Crawling practice and use of ground.
	1700	Lecture : " German Organization."
5th day	0900—1215	In the field. Observation—Magnetic bearings—Practical use of protractor—Map reading — Pin pointing of positions—Resection.
	1400—1600	Same as morning.
	2200	Night Patrol Scheme.

6th day	0900—1215	Observation—Demonstration—Model German trench—Spotting prepared movement—Snipers—Observers—Dummies—Periscopes—Machine guns—Saps. Followed by Camouflage—Demonstration and use of dummy heads.
	1400—1500	Preparing Report with map or sketch from notes taken during morning.
	1500—1600	Enlargement of map squares—B.27, 28—H.3. 4 to 1/10,000—Ref. Map 44B. 1/40,000.
	1700	Lecture.
7th day	All day	Reconnaissance—Tactical Exercise: Open Warfare. To practise scoutcraft—Observation — Use of ground—Map reading—Bearings—Reports, topography, etc.
	1700	Complete report on day's work.
8th day	0900—1215	Organization of Brigade and Battalion Front Line Intelligence in detail, with diagrams and system of collecting, reporting and summarizing information from observation posts, scouts, snipers, etc.
	1400—1600	Map reading—Exercise on prepared contours.
	1700	Lecture: " Aeroplane Photographs."
9th day	All day	Reconnaissance: Tactical Scheme. Same as 7th day, but positions reversed. Attack now becomes defence.
10th day	0900—1215	Lecture and Break: " Handing-Over Reports and Working Maps. Conventional Signs."
	1400—1600	Class to prepare Handing-Over Report and Working Maps.
11th day	0900	General discussion of past ten days' work.

Lightning Source UK Ltd.
Milton Keynes UK
UKHW020657230320
360738UK00002B/10